beLEEve

A Journey of Loss, Healing and Hope

Rosanne Groover Norris

beLEEve: A Journey of Loss, Healing and Hope

As You Wish Publishing, LLC
Connect@asyouwishpublishing.com
www.asyouwishpublishing.com

ISBN-13: 978-1-951131-05-0

Library of Congress Control Number: 2020911760

Edited by Todd Schaefer

Printed in the United States of America.

Nothing in this book or any affiliations with this book is a substitute for medical or psychological help. If you are needing help please seek it.

This book is dedicated to my son, Lee Thomas Norris (9/7/87–1/9/18), and his dog, Buddy, who passed two days after Lee. I am grateful you chose me to be your mom, and I had you in my life for thirty years.

I look forward to our adventures together when it's my turn to cross.

I love you with all my broken heart!

Mom

Table Of Contents

Foreword i

YEAR ONE 1

    The Beginning 3

    The Day 4

    Lee 8

    Siblings 14

    The Last Contact 16

    The Services 18

    Accidents 20

    The First Year 22

    January 2018 23

    February 2018 28

    March 2018 37

    April 2018 45

    May 2018 52

    June 2018 61

    July 2018 66

    August 2018 74

    September 2018 82

    October 2018 95

    November 2018 108

    December 2018 119

YEAR TWO 131

January 2019 133

February 2019 148

March 2019 159

April 2019 173

May 2019.. 182

June 2019.. 195

July 2019 204

August 2019 212

September 2019.. 220

October 2019.. 227

November 2019... 232

December 2019 240

January 2020 248

Lee's Favorite Recipes 251

Afterword.. 253

Acknowledgments.. 255

About the Author 257

Foreword

Rosanne and I met in the fall of 2018. She reached out requesting a private reading, and I promptly scheduled her session. From the moment I heard her voice, I knew this reading was going to be special. Working with those who are grieving the loss of a loved one is rewarding, and with it comes tremendous responsibility. My time with Rosanne was mutually respectful and filled with the emotions of tears and laughter as if we'd known each other for decades.

I recall when Lee expressed to me that he was encouraging her to write a book and that the signs he was sending were genuine. Lee understood this would be incredibly difficult for his mother. Yet, he also knew that it would be a significant aspect of her healing. The journal entries that were once known only to this devoted mother are meant to provide a glimpse into the reality that follows the transition of a child to the Spirit world. Rosanne's words are raw, heartfelt, and filled with the anger and sorrow one would expect, yet there is also hope. The promise that beyond the pain is a new connection between souls that is yet to be fully discovered. This hope builds anticipation and encouragement for the reunion that will ultimately take place between mother and son. Rosanne's ability to express the most vulnerable parts of her journey makes this book a blessing for anyone who is experiencing loss of the physical bond.

Reading Rosanne's book reminds me that the veil between this world and the next is much thinner than we might realize. Even though I communicate with Spirit, I am continually amazed and delighted at the evidence that exists if we are willing to awaken our awareness. I give thanks to Rosanne and Lee for trusting me with their sacred connection and to Spirit for showing me that love is and always will be the oneness that binds us for eternity.

With gratitude,

Ann Van Orsdel

YEAR
ONE

The Beginning

What the hell just happened? How did this happen? Why? Where have you gone?

This is a journey I never expected to be on. What parent does? Lee's death left me reeling, grasping for answers. It seemed so senseless and pointless. I couldn't accept he was gone and buried in the ground. Where was my beautiful redheaded boy now that he wasn't in his body? I couldn't imagine he wouldn't walk through my door and sit at the counter for a meal. Or sit out back and watch a sporting event with his dad, and his dog Buddy, on his lap. I couldn't accept he was gone forever.

He had to be somewhere. I had to know where he was and if he was okay. I had to have answers. I had to have proof Lee still existed. And so, I began my journey. And I found my proof. Energy cannot be destroyed. Lee is alive!

This is the first two years of my grief journey and awakening, a kind of spiritual rags to riches story. It's a journey of two steps forward, one step back and sometimes four back, but one I will continue. I am determined to heal.

I've always loved to write and hoped to write a book someday, but I never imagined writing this book. Some of you may not like or believe my story because you don't understand. You're not meant to. But it's my story, my journey and I will tell it as I understand it. And if it helps one person through this roller coaster ride called grief, then I've accomplished something grand in my life. I beLEEve!

The Day

Tuesday, January 9, 2018, 1:30 p.m.

My phone rang at work.

Lee's boss called. "He did not show up for work today, and he wasn't in yesterday either," my husband, Tom, said.

In that instant, I knew.

I grabbed my purse and coat on the way out the door. My knees buckled as I told my boss I had to go.

"Lee is gone," I yelled and ran from the building.

I arrived at Lee's house in 10 minutes and waited for Tom, not daring to go in by myself. He showed up a few minutes later. It was 1:45 p.m.

Tom unlocked the door, and I followed him inside. The smell of dog feces was strong. Lee was lying on his couch with a blanket pulled up around his neck. He looked like he was sleeping.

I ran to the couch and touched his cheek. It was cold. I dropped to the floor and screamed.

The desperation in Tom's voice forced me to get up as he shook Lee and pounded on his chest, saying "Lee wake up. Wake up."

"Stop. Please stop," I begged. "He's gone."

I stroked Lee's face, hair, and beard as Tom made the 911 call. Then we heard a small noise from somewhere in the house.

"The dog?" I looked at the cage. Buddy was not there. We started to look around, but the noise had stopped. Right then, I couldn't care less about the dog. My son was lying on his couch where he died and laid alone for at least a day or two. I returned to Lee.

There was a knock at the door, and when I answered, two men stood there. I was confused and thought they might be friends dropping by. For a moment, I felt annoyed, like Lee had skipped work and these guys had stopped by for some fun. I wish. I asked them if they knew my son, but they said no.

"Who are you?"

"Volunteer firemen."

And then it began. So many people showed up as I continued to sit by Lee. They walked around the house as I kept my post next to Lee.

A trooper came over to the couch, stood there for a moment, then asked, "Is that marijuana?" pointing to a small pile the size of a dime. My son is dead, and this was all he could say? I wanted to scream.

We heard a small noise, and the trooper went to investigate. He returned and said he found a dog in the back bedroom. I followed him and picked up Buddy. He was limp in my arms, but alive. He sipped a little water then I laid him inside his kennel and returned to Lee. Buddy passed a day later. He was a tiny dog. How could he have survived the poison that took Lee's life? I believe he watched over Lee until we found him.

Then I was told I had to leave immediately. The level of carbon monoxide was dangerously high. They asked how long we had been in the house and if I felt nauseous or had a headache. My son was dead, and my world had shattered. A headache? Nausea? I wish. But I felt nothing. I was numb with shock and disbelief as someone led me from the house.

It was a bitter, cold day. I was put in a warm vehicle. A man introduced himself and said he had to ask some questions. Tom was questioned in another vehicle. We were questioned over and over by different people, all writing things down for their reports. I have no idea what I said. Time had stopped.

My brother called while I sat there. I remember yelling into the phone, "Lee is dead, Lee is dead," over and over. He kept asking, "What?" I'm sure he was trying to process what I had just said.

It wasn't long before two of my brothers showed up. Tom had made the painful phone calls to Lee's two brothers, Todd and Jay. That only left April and Anna to be told the devastating news.

My brothers left to pick up April from work. When they returned, they put her in the car with me. She was hysterical, and we clung to each other. We waited for someone to tell us what we were supposed to do. It was unreal. My mind had shut down.

Our youngest daughter, Anna, was returning from Florida, having spent a week with her cousin. There was no way to contact her, and as this was not the news we wanted to divulge over the phone, we decided to wait until she arrived, in Binghamton, late that night.

After who knows how long, I was taken home. Phone calls were made. Family came. Everything was a blur.

"What is going on? What is happening? This can't be real. It doesn't feel real." I kept asking this over and over while walking around in a stupor.

Then April took charge. I remember thinking, "I'm the mom. I'm supposed to take care of everyone." But I was completely helpless. She called my doctor to ask for medication to help me. For anyone that knows me, I am an anti-pill person. It's hard for me to even take an aspirin. Though I admit, the wine was going down my throat quite easily, to not feel this pain or anything at all.

The time was dragging as we waited to go to the airport to meet Anna. My phone rang. It was Anna calling from the Atlanta airport. Unfortunately, someone had sent her a text saying they were sorry to hear about Lee.

"It's not true. Tell me it's not true," she said.

"I'm so sorry," I told her. "We were waiting until you got to Binghamton to tell you. You weren't supposed to find out like this."

Then I heard the most primordial scream I have ever heard. It was gut-wrenching and tore my heart out. I will never forget the sounds coming over my phone as long as I live. And there was nothing I could do. She was hundreds of miles away and still had a layover before she would arrive home.

Then a bathroom attendant was on the phone with me. I told her what had happened.

"Can you please take her to the Delta counter and ask them to help her? Can you take care of my daughter?"

She promised she would and told me how sorry she was for my loss. It was hard to break the connection to Anna. I felt so helpless knowing she was alone with this crushing news.

Anna was taken to the Delta counter and handed over to their care. They put her in a private room until it was time to board, then she was escorted to a first-class seat for the two-hour flight to Detroit. Once there, she was again taken to a room to wait for her final flight home, where she was met by her uncles. She arrived home around midnight. By then, Lee had been gone from our lives for over ten hours.

Lee

Lee was my fourth child, and the only one I knew the gender before birth, although a big surprise was in store. A week before he was born, in the shower, a sense of dread came over me. I started to cry and was scared.

"I don't want to do this," I thought to myself.

Then I felt silly. I had birthed babies before. I knew Lee was going to be a big baby. My three before him were all 9 pounders.

So, what was it that put me on edge? As I look back on it now, I wonder, did my soul know?

Lee was born on Labor Day, September 7, 1987, weighing in at 11 pounds, 3 ounces, and 23 inches in length. He was the largest baby born naturally, at the hospital, a record he held for many years and may still. Lee was reluctant to be born, but after eleven difficult hours, he arrived. It had been a traumatic event for us all. But the trauma soon was forgotten when Lee was placed in my arms. He was plump, blue-eyed, and had gorgeous red hair. I looked at my large, beautiful baby and was filled with love.

As a baby, Lee looked like a little white Buddha. When placed on his back, he was like a turtle, too large to roll over until he was a year old. He was slow to walk, almost 18 months. But despite his large size at birth, Lee was small growing up.

As a child, Lee was different from his four siblings. He was quiet, sensitive, introspective, and cried easily. At night, I would sing songs like "You Are My Sunshine" and "Go to Sleep Little Lamb," and Lee would cry. I would ask him why he cried, and he would say, "The songs make me sad." He was the only one of my children to carry a security item, a little stuffed bear we called Beaners. He clutched Beaners all the time, but he was always willing to share it with his little sister, Anna. Beaners now sits on my altar where I meditate.

Lee was a daddy's boy. Anytime he got hurt, he would go to his father for comfort. And he loved to dress up in his daddy's clothes.

Lee was kind. One act of kindness I recall was when he was in high school working concessions at the local arena. When he learned one of his co-workers worked a full-time job in addition to the part-time one, often working 13 to 14 hours a day, Lee gave the man all the tips he earned. Lee said he couldn't take his share of the tips when the man was trying to feed his family.

Growing up, Lee played baseball, basketball, football, and golf. I spent many years on benches watching him play. His dad spent many years coaching some of his teams. These were good years. In college, he took up broomball, a crazy game of running on ice, hitting a ball with a stick, called a broom. His hockey-playing best friend, Justin, nicknamed, JT, would tease him about this game. He continued to play softball and flag football for a time, but Lee soon became a fairly well-known gamer under the name *Leeweasley*, a pastime he had started in his youth. Lee also had great rhythm and was a good dancer. I only got to dance with him once at a family friend's wedding, a memory I will cherish forever.

Lee loved to eat. It was serious business to him. When he was a little boy, his head would go down at the table, and it wouldn't come up until he was finished. He would try anything and liked almost everything, but oddly enough, he didn't like peas or lima beans, and neither do I. New England Clam Chowder became his adult favorite. He was always my taster and would let me know if my soup needed anything. Hummus became another favorite. Lee told me to include both recipes, which I have at the end of the book.

Lee had a great work ethic, but never gave himself enough credit. Due to his small size, he didn't excel in sports, like basketball or football, but he never missed a practice, and he gave it his all. However, he was a very good baseball player, batting clean-up in high school. He also did well in school and earned a scholarship to Clarkson University, one of the top private engineering schools in New York State. He made the Dean's and President's list several semesters. And during his five-year career with BAE Systems, an aerospace company, Lee was recognized several times with monetary awards for his accomplishhments. He had a bright future ahead of him, and yet, he never felt he was good enough.

Lee was a private, deep thinker, and loved to read. He loved anything to do with space and the stars. We used to lie in the backyard watching for shooting stars in the summer. He also loved shows about the earth and animals. He was a big Stephen King fan until he discovered George R. R. Martin, who he thought was brilliant. If you brought up a subject Lee loved, he would become animated talking about it. I treasure these memories.

Lee was quiet and serious, but once you got to know him, he showed his funny and silly side, but sometimes he could also be moody, and he would mutter under his breath. Later a dark side would emerge. While in college, Lee started using Adderall. He said it was to help him focus. I warned him about the dangers of using a drug not prescribed to him, but he blew me off, saying it was no big deal. I'm sorry to say I backed down, hoping for the best. But after college, we noticed some behavioral changes in him. He had anxiety and depression issues. I'm not sure if this was caused by the drug, but there were a few very scary moments with Lee. At one point, I asked him if he wanted to kill himself, and he said, "Every day, but I would never do that to you." Those were the most frightening words I had ever heard. I had no idea how to deal with this, and as Lee was an adult, I had little recourse. But if I am honest with myself, what I did was bury my head in the sand, and hope for the best. And I watched. When his live-in girlfriend left him in the spring of 2017, I was afraid he would go off the deep end, but that didn't happen. He had stopped using the Adderall and started working out. Then in the fall of 2017, Lee told me, "I'm the happiest I've been in a long time."

Thinking back on those words, I now believe Lee had completed what he came here to do and learn, which brings me far more comfort than thinking his death was a senseless accident. I believe his soul took an opportunity or exit point to help him leave, maybe early, but gently. Who knows what may have been lurking just around the corner?

Siblings

Lee's two oldest siblings were from my first marriage. Todd was thirteen when Lee was born and April, eleven. Next is Jay, two years older than Lee. Two years after Lee, Anna came along.

Those early years were crazy juggling five kids, with such a large gap in age. Tom worked the swing shift, six or seven days a week, to keep the family afloat. Additionally, he had gone back to school for engineering to give him an edge at work, even though he already had a four-year degree. I spent my days cooking, feeding, and caring for Jay, Lee, and Anna, plus preparing for outings to the various ball games and other activities Todd and April were involved in.

Lee looked up to Jay and was into whatever Jay was into, like Ninja Turtles, video games, and sports. Because they looked a lot alike, in school, Lee was called "Little Jay." After college, Lee and Jay became even closer, spending a lot of time together, going to concerts, sporting events, or just hanging out. When they were together, there was a lot of laughter and teasing banter that only siblings can do. I loved listening to that banter.

When Anna came along, Lee just loved her. He liked to hold her and would share his Beaners with her. He would get in her playpen (yes, I used one) and contentedly play with her.

In the summer of 1992, we gained a special addition to our family. Lawrence Harper came to us through the Fresh Air Fund, a program for inner-city kids to experience a more rural life. Lawrence was six years old at the time, and what started as a two-week visit grew to whole summers and Christmas visits. I fondly call him my "summer son," and he calls me "Mom." Lawrence is and will always be Lee's brother and part of our family.

Lee was close to his four siblings, and they got along well. Lee loved kids and adored his nephew, Luke, and five nieces, Hailey, Ella, Ava, Harper, and Haydan. There wasn't one family party where you wouldn't find Lee, all sweaty, under a pile of those kids.

The Last Contact

There was a persistent arctic blast, in the northeast, which lasted from late December into January. I invited Lee for dinner on January 1, but since he had been with us the night before, he took a pass.

Lee texted me on Wednesday, January 3, at 10:37 a.m.

"Just got a date for Sunday."

"How exciting."

This would be Lee's first date since the break-up of his five-year relationship six months before.

He sent me a picture of a dark-haired beauty.

"We've been talking the past couple of days. She's very pretty."

"Hopefully, she's as nice as she is pretty."

"She seems nice, so far. We shall see."

"I'm glad you are ready to date."

End of communication.

Friday, January 5, 9:13 a.m.

My text to Lee:

"Used the gift certificate last night."

"Awesome. Hope it was a good dinner. I'm sure it was."

"It was. Thanks for the gift."

Friday, January 5, 8:49 p.m.

"How you doing in this freeze?" I texted to Lee.

"Fine. It's 70 in here."

No further texts that night.

Saturday, January 6, 6:59 p.m.

"Date still on for tomorrow?" I ask.

"Yep."

"Oh, good. Where you going?"

"The Colonial."

"Good first date."

"Should be fun."

"Casual and relaxed."

There was no response, but I had no cause to worry. I couldn't wait to hear about the date even though Tom had cautioned me not to bug him about it.

Lee never showed for his date set for 6 p.m.

I later found a text on Lee's phone telling him how rude and disrespectful he was for standing her up. I'm sure she felt terrible once she heard. I wish she could have seen for herself the kind, witty, silly, and smart person Lee was. I know she would have liked him.

Lee was supposed to play Fortnite with his buddies that night. He told his college buddy, JT, he had a headache and was going to lie down. It was 10:30 p.m.

Lee never got online.

Sunday, January 7, 12:24 p.m.

"Have you tried your new crockpot yet?"

No response.

Monday, January 8, 9:23 a.m.

"How did the date go?"

No response.

I wasn't concerned with the lack of response. It was a workday, and he had just started a new position in his company. He was very excited about this new opportunity.

Tuesday, January 9, 8:49 a.m.

"Just checking if I am on for Buddy?"

I would let out Lee's dog, Buddy, on Tuesdays, because he bowled after work. Lee didn't respond, which I found unsettling, but I ignored my uneasy feeling.

1:30 p.m.

Tom calls, and our world shatters.

The Services

I don't recall much about the viewing and funeral. So many decisions had to be made. Thankfully, Tom took care of everything. I was quite incapable.

The funeral director said the viewing was one of the largest ever held there. I don't know how I stood for the four-plus hours while people filed through, but I did. I later learned angels were holding me up.

My mind and body were under the influence of Xanax. Otherwise, I would have been a heap on the floor. I knew I was acting like a dull zombie, but I didn't care. "Thank you for coming," was all I could manage to say to each person.

I remember very few people who attended. Only two people sparked a reaction in me. The first was Lawrence, who came into the room to take his place with the family. I flew to his side and clung to him, sobbing. He and his fiancé had traveled, by bus, from New York to say their goodbyes to Lee. The other person was JT. There was an obvious bond of brotherly love between JT and Lee. The pain on JT's face was excruciating to see as I watched him place a fraternity paddle in the casket with Lee.

I did notice how perfect Lee looked. Later, in a reading, Lee said he was standing behind me, with the angels. He commented on how good he thought he looked.

The funeral was the next day, and again I was in a Xanax haze. I could sense the fullness of the church, but I couldn't see the faces. I recall nothing of the Mass. The priest's words were garbled, and the music made me sick to my stomach. I just sat there waiting for it to be over.

It's funny the things you do remember, though. As we drove from the church to the cemetery, I noticed several intersections were blocked off by police cars. I remember thinking, "Something big must be happening." Later, I learned nearly every police officer, both on and off duty, volunteered to stand watch over the funeral procession, in honor, of the nephew of one of their own.

It was another brutally cold day, and it took quite a while for everyone to make their way into the tiny, rural cemetery. The wind was fierce, but I felt nothing. I wanted to feel nothing. I wanted to be nothing. I wanted to trade places with Lee. I wanted to be dead.

After, we gathered at a local Irish bar. The place was packed with family and friends. Lee's friends from high school were there, plus several college fraternity buddies who flew in from all over the country. The frat boys sang their rowdy fraternity songs over and over and toasted their brother, Lee.

Accidents

We called him "Lucky Lee," but he wasn't. Accidents, large and small, seemed to happen to Lee, and now I wonder if the accidents were a foreshadowing of the final accident that took his life.

He was around sixteen months and not yet walking. He moved around the house on a little scooter. One day, he scooted into the kitchen, hit the basement door, and rode the stairs all the way to the bottom. He was crying, but miraculously unharmed. Tom immediately changed the door to open into the kitchen and put a latch on it for an extra measure of safety. I think how easily his life could have ended that day.

At age four, he fell against our coffee table and cut his nose severely, requiring three layers of stitches. Not fatal but traumatic, nonetheless.

A near-miss I witnessed happened when Lee was about twelve. I was in the yard when I heard, "Mom, watch." I looked up the hill in time to see Lee careening down, on his new Razor, at a ridiculous speed. He had no helmet or pads on. I envisioned him hitting the smallest pebble and spattered on the road. Or worse, making to the blind curve only to be struck by a vehicle. I felt sick to my stomach and had to turn away, not wanting to witness either of the choices that came to mind. Somehow, he managed to navigate into the driveway and onto the lawn. You can imagine the words I had for him.

Another accident happened in football practice in ninth grade. Lee's thumb was severely dislocated, and it took two doctors to get it back in place. When he returned to football, he took a hard hit and cracked a rib, but he never told anyone. I only found out years later when he had an x-ray to diagnose a back problem.

In 2010, in the spring semester of his senior year at college, Lee had two significant accidents. The first involved an ultimate fighter, who demonstrated a chokehold on Lee, paralyzing him, from the neck down. He was taken to the hospital by ambulance, where the doctor's determined the paralysis was temporary. We got the call around 1 a.m., never a good time with kids. After a few hours, he regained full movement. There were plenty of smiling pictures on Facebook, one with a container of urine, which Lee and his buddies found hysterical. Later, Lee admitted he was so scared, and sure he was paralyzed for life. I was simply grateful his neck wasn't snapped. A month later, Lee fell down the basement stairs and broke his two front teeth, which prompted another trip to the emergency room and another call in the middle of the night. When he told me what happened, I asked, "Were you drinking?" Lee replied, "Duh. Of course, I was drinking." I remembered going down those narrow, steep steps into the basement where the brothers held parties and played games. I'm sure Lee wasn't the first person to take a tumble down those treacherous steps.

The last incident happened in 2016 with Jay. They had attended a concert and had booked a hotel room, but decided not to stay. Jay was driving and fell asleep, hitting the center guard rail. They were not hurt. Lee took charge of the situation, making phone calls for a tow truck and a pick up from a friend. Their cover story was that a deer ran in front of the car. I knew it wasn't true, and after Lee passed, Jay admitted falling asleep. I thought about how I could have lost both boys that night.

The First Year

I wrote five journals in the first year. The pain was immense and all-consuming, especially in the first few months. It was physically, mentally, and emotionally exhausting. I existed in a fog. I couldn't swim out of it. (They call it grief brain.) On the good days, I sat and stared or wandered around the house. Other times, I curled up in a ball, crying and screaming. The only way to escape the pain was to sleep or die. I preferred the latter, but unless I took action, it wasn't going to be the way out. However, I understand why parents choose to follow their kids, but unless you have walked in our shoes, you wouldn't understand. I pray, you never know.

My emotions bounced all over the place, shifting from day to day, hour to hour, or even minute to minute. I felt like I was dragging a ball and chain tethered to my heart. Grief from child loss is the hardest work you'll ever do.

January 2018

Saturday, January 20

Dear Lee,

BLACK HOLE.

It feels like this is where you went, but it's just my heart. I know God took you for a reason. At least that's what I'm supposed to believe, but I wish he would tell me why. I've decided to try church and see if he might tell me. He probably won't because it's supposed to be a mystery, which seems pretty ridiculous. You're just supposed to have faith. I want it, because if I don't have faith, then I feel like I won't have you. So, I'm going to try.

Love, Mom

Sunday, January 21

Dear Lee,

Church did not go well.

Love, Mom

Monday, January 22

Dear Lee,

I returned to work today, but I mostly sat and stared. My co-workers are like extended family, so it was easy to be with them. I came home from work exhausted and felt myself sinking hard. I asked you for a sign as I sat looking at your picture. I started to heat some leftovers and decided to turn on the television for noise. Dr. Oz introduced his show about life after death. Is this a sign?

The show featured two non-believing, hard-core scientists, Dr. Eben Alexander and Dr. Mary Neal. They each had a near-death experience that changed their lives. And they were about to change mine.

The show ended, and I had a moment where I imagined you being welcomed to the other side by family and friends who were looking at us, foolishly crying when you were perfectly fine. I know this isn't a magic bullet. I know there is no on and off switch for grief. I know I have a long way to go and a lot of work ahead of me, but it's a start, right? I just had my first glimpse of hope, a tiny ray in the distance to focus on. And I promise you as things get a little easier, I will live large for you. I promise with all my heart. I love you, and miss you terribly.

Love, Mom

Tuesday, January 23

Dear Lee,

I understand mothers and fathers grieve differently. Dad wants to get rid of everything and sell the house. I want to go slow, process, and grieve. I can't think straight, and this is all too much.

Love, Mom

Wednesday, January 24

Dear Lee,

It's a bad day today. I know you don't like seeing me in so much pain. I try to tell myself you are safe and happy, but it's not working. I know your death was painless. You just went to sleep, but why wasn't your device on the wall? Why did you take it down? I am angry at you for this. And I hate your coal furnace. I wanted to kick it, but I'd probably break my toe. I love you, and miss you terribly.

Love, Mom

Thursday, January 25

Dear Lee,

Dr. Alexander's book came today. I will dive right in and look for answers.

Love, Mom

Friday, January 26

Dear Lee,

I met an angel today.

Ernie is a former preacher who has counseled grief-stricken people over forty-plus years, only accepting free-will donations. I asked how he could take on so much grief for so many decades, and he said, "I have no choice. I was called by God." Ernie is a large, charismatic man with a deep booming voice, but a gentleness that makes you feel safe and protected. He said he was impressed I had come to him so early in my grief. "I can't do this alone," I told him. He explained the shock phase and said to be gentle with myself and only do what I could manage. He said I was "ahead of the curve." I have no idea what he means, and I certainly don't feel ahead of any curve. He also said, "It's a shitty club." That I get. Ernie said to "Get in and get out." He said to feel the emotions fully, then let them go and take a walk, listen to music, or do whatever soothes me. What would soothe me is to be with you.

Love, Mom

Saturday, January 27

I HATE THIS FUCKING CLUB!

Love, Mom

Sunday, January 28

Dear Lee,

I haven't been to your gravesite yet. I don't know when I can. I know you aren't there, but I'm not ready. We need to order a headstone too, but it's too much.

Love, Mom

Monday, January 29

Dear Lee,

Maybe I'll get a tattoo. I feel like I have a phantom limb from you being ripped from me, so if I put something permanent on my body, maybe you will always be with me.

Love always, Mom

Tuesday, January 30

Dear Lee,

Can't sleep. I imagined you gaming, laughing, and drinking margaritas. Did you like margaritas? Buddy was happily playing near you. At least you are happy.

Love, Mom

Wednesday, January 31 (5:21 a.m.)

Dear Lee,

I'm up to watch the Super Moon with you but from different places. I wonder how it looks from your perspective. You loved the stars. Not long ago, you had your telescope out to look at the moon. I wish we had done it more. It seemed like we had forever then.

9:45 p.m.

I no longer fit in. I hear people complain about things and I scream inside, "MY SON IS DEAD." This isn't just a shitty club, it's a fucking prison.

Love, Mom

February 2018

Thursday, February 1

Dear Lee,

What was our last conversation? I can't remember. I wish it was imprinted on my mind. It was hard to draw you out unless it was something that interested you. I loved it when you talked about Game of Thrones, Stephen King, the Planet Earth series, gaming, or anything related to the stars and cosmos. Then you talked a blue streak. Otherwise, you would try to blend in or recede to the background, even in family situations. Did you notice me watching you your last few months on earth? I can't explain it, and I tried to be discreet, but I felt I needed to watch you. Maybe my soul knew. (In a reading, Lee disclosed he knew I was watching him.)

Dad called from work to tell me there's a new driver in NASCAR. Michael McDowell drives car number 34. (Lee's youth football number will start to show up frequently). It's his new guy.

Love, Mom

Friday, February 2

It's Ground Hog Day and exactly how I feel. I wake up and have to live the pain and horror over and over.

Love, Mom

Saturday, February 3

Dear Lee,

A dime rolled under my dresser, and when I pulled it out, I found a second dime. I hope it's a sign. I haven't listened to music, but I decide to turn on the radio in the car and an Offspring song is playing. You loved that band when you were a teen. This is definitely a sign.

Love, Mom

Sunday, February 4

Dear Lee,

I pull out Offspring's Greatest Hits from a box in your basement. And I hear, "I'm okay, Mom. I'm fine." Am I making this up?

Our first family dinner is today at 2 p.m. I want to call it off, but it's catered, so I can't. I think I'm having a panic attack. I've never had one before.

Dinner was awkward. Your death has ripped a hole in the fabric of our family.

Love, Mom

Monday, February 5

Dear Lee,

I handed in my retirement notice today. I need to be alone. I can't exist in everyone's normal. I need time to explore and learn about the afterlife.

Love, Mom

Tuesday, February 6

Dear Lee,

I felt a nudge to play my friend's music this morning, then found out he died tonight. I picture him playing his sax in Heaven.

I finished *Proof of Heaven* tonight. It gives me hope. I crave more. I need to know.

Love, Mom

Wednesday, February 7

Dear Lee,

Something inside me says you had to go. Ernie says there are no accidents. Please help me understand.

Love, Mom

Thursday, February 8

Dear Lee,

I woke up around midnight from a dream. I saw a balcony with lots of people on it. You were front and center. Redheads can never hide in a crowd.

Love, Mom

Friday, February 9

Dear Lee,

It's funny how things are put into your path at just the right time. I'm watching a band unload from my hotel window. (I bought tickets in November, so we decided to go.) I pull open the nightstand drawer and find Vincent Norman Peale's book, *The Power of Positive Thinking*. This isn't the typical material found in a hotel room. I scan the table of contents and see the chapter, "The Prescription for

Heartache." Peale talks about dying people, who see their loved ones, who have passed. I felt a little like the Grinch when his heart grew. I felt a shift and a tiny smidge of peace in my heart. I know I have a long way to go and will never be the same, but I will heal this giant hole in my heart. I know I am a broken person, but I promise to be a better person. And I will thank God every day for giving you to me for thirty years.

Love, Mom

Saturday, February 10

Dear Lee,

Remember the fort we made in the woods together? I think it was the only fort I made in my life. I'm so glad it was with you.

Love, Mom

Sunday, February 11

Dear Lee,

I heard Dad muttering to himself this morning. You used to mutter. Now you have no reason to.

Love, Mom

Monday, February 12

Dear Lee,

This day started okay, but then I watched a family video that cut my legs out from under me. Now breathing is hard, and I feel like I am dragging a weight. I wish the weight was you, but in a way, it is.

Love, Mom

Tuesday, February 13

Dear Lee,

Tuesdays are tough. I tried to ignore the time, but my eyes get drawn to the clock. Then all I can see is you dead on your couch. What did it feel like to leave your body? Did you know immediately? Were you scared? Was someone who loves you there to greet you? Did you want to go with them or were you sad to leave your family and friends? I focus on the fact I had you for thirty years. Other mothers didn't get that much time. I think of those mothers whose children felt terror or pain. You simply fell asleep. I'll try to be grateful—all those grieving mothers. I don't know them, and yet I know them all.

Love, Mom

Wednesday, February 14

Dear Lee,

It's Valentine's Day. This is the worst I've felt. The scab is off, and the pain is shocking. I had no idea I could suffer this much. Torture could not be worse than this.

Love, Mom

Thursday, February 15 (9:30 p.m.)

Dear Lee,

Every day seems endless. I hope 2018 passes quickly, so maybe this pain will ease a little. I look at the calendar, and it's only been six weeks. How can time be such a blur and yet drag so slowly?

Love, Mom

Saturday, February 17

Dear Lee,

I know this was an accident, but why did you have to be so careless?

Love, Mom

Sunday, February 18

Dear Lee,

WHY IS TIME MOVING SO SLOWLY?

Love, Mom

Monday, February 19

Dear Lee,

Today I feel angry. I'm so angry with you. Why did you remove the detector from the wall? I'm angry because everyone is so normal and happy. And I hear in my head, "I'm fine, Mom. I'm free." And I hate that because I want you here, not wherever you are. And I'm scared because what if you are just dead in the ground and that's it? But there has to be more, otherwise, what is the point of everything?

Love, Mom

Tuesday, February 20

Dear Lee,

Today I dumped coins in a coin return. Two dimes were rejected. What are the chances?

Love, Mom

Wednesday, February 21

Dear Lee,

I managed ten minutes on the treadmill this morning. My body is hurting from the lack of exercise. When I was on the treadmill, I had a moment where I felt a fleeting little nudge of acceptance. Were you prompting me? Was God?

Love, Mom

Thursday, February 22

One day keeps turning into the next, but still, time moves so slowly. Everything is so hazy and fragmented in my mind. I want to go back to sleep, so I don't have to think or feel. I want to be alone. I want to sit quietly. I don't want to see people.

The news is unbearable. Parents lose their kids to violence, and I think, "Who am I to complain?" At least you didn't suffer.

I've been sleeping with your green sweater. It still has your smell on it, but for how long? I loved you in that sweater. Is that why you often wore it when you came for dinner?

Love, Mom

Sunday, February 25

Dear Lee,

Last fall, I dreamed you died two or three times. It was awful. But the worst one was when I saw you in a casket wearing the green sweater. Why did I dream that? What good did it do? I didn't save you, and it didn't prepare me in any way, so why? Was I supposed to do something and failed? Why didn't I feel something was wrong? I hate your furnace, and I hate that you are gone. If you were here now, what would you say to me? Probably how sorry you are that we are all hurting so much. I know you never meant to cause us this pain. If only you had realized something was wrong. If only you had taken Buddy outside. **IF ONLY** doesn't matter. **WHAT IS,** is the reality. You always seemed to get the short end of the stick, but no matter what, you sucked it up and carried on.

Love, Mom

Monday, February 26

Dear Lee,

Dad is beating himself up about not asking questions about your furnace. I tell him it's not his fault. You were thirty years old and owned a home. You were supposed to be a responsible adult. But Dad always asked those kinds of questions. Am I angry at him? Do I blame him a little bit? I'm too exhausted to figure it out right now. Inside my head is a scream, "MY SON IS DEAD." What am I going to do? How can I fix this hole? How much can I take before I crack wide open and fall into an abyss from which I may not return? I think of all the mothers who have done this. How?

Love, Mom

Tuesday, February 27

Dear Lee,

I thought I'd be a mess today because it's Tuesday, but I wasn't until I spotted a sign offering free carbon monoxide testing. It was a punch in the gut.

Love, Mom

Wednesday, February 28

Dear Lee,

I am afraid I might lose another child. When Anna didn't return my text, I thought, "What if she is dead in her apartment?" What if something bad happens and I lose someone else? I feel scared, angry, and sad, all at once. Why was your detector down? Why didn't Dad tell you to get your furnace checked? Why did this happen? Why do I want to scream at everyone? Why did I have the dream? Why couldn't I save you? Why did you have to die? I am suffocating.

Love, Mom

March 2018

Thursday, March 1

Dear Lee,

I saw a priest today, and he asked me if God came to me when I was pregnant and said I would have a wonderful, smart, handsome and successful boy, but he would take you away in thirty years, would I agree to those terms? I said, "Yes." He said he never met a mom who said otherwise. I wanted to ask him if God took you and why, but I was afraid of what he might say. Did God take you? If so, then I am angry at God. I told him about my dream and asked if he thought it was a premonition. He said it wasn't a premonition, only my fears talking. The priest was not helpful. It felt rote, like confession. Say ten Our Father's, and all will be well.

Love, Mom

Friday, March 2

Dear Lee,

I am having a very bad day. Crying, yelling, and screaming. I feel it in my chest. I miss you so much. I feel robbed. I feel cheated. I feel gutted. I feel amputated. I feel violated. I feel wronged. I feel pain. I feel sad. I feel alone. I feel lost. I feel empty.

Love, Mom

Saturday, March 3

Dear Lee,

I'm reading *On Grief and Grieving* by Elizabeth Kubler Ross and David Kessler. I read about regrets, and I thought about mine.

I regret never having dinner with you at your house.

I regret not spending time with you at your house, even if you were playing video games.

I regret not asking how you were feeling.

I regret assuming you were okay because I was too scared to know.

I regret not playing more games with you.

I regret not insisting that you come to dinner even when you said you were too busy.

I regret not mentioning I smelled rotten eggs in your house for two weeks before you passed.

Regrets, oh yeah, I have a few.

Love, Mom

Sunday, March 4

Dear Lee,

Dad discovered the blockage in your furnace. He wonders why he didn't tell you to have it cleaned or if he did, why you didn't listen. Does it matter? It doesn't change anything. The blockage is there. The door, on the furnace, wasn't closed properly. The detector was off the wall. It was a perfect storm, and now you are dead. And the old me is dead too. I will never be the same person again. Ernie tells me I will be stretched and will become a different person. And I will emerge a better person. I thought I was a pretty good person, but I guess I was wrong.

Love, Mom

Monday, March 5

Dear Lee,

Dad and Todd both blame themselves, and it makes me mad. They take it upon themselves when it's on you. What was so important you couldn't be bothered to clean your coal furnace? You were careless, and now your dad and brother feel bad because of your stupid carelessness. You make me so angry. Your carelessness cost you your life and robbed us of you. I wish you could explain the detector. Why Lee?

Love, Mom

Ernie suggested I write a *Dear Mom* letter.

Dear Mom,

I wish I could take it all back. I wish I could take away everyone's pain. I don't like to see you hurting so much. I'm sorry. I would change it if I could. Yes, I was careless but not purposely. I was lazy and distracted, but it was not intentional. I love you very much, and I am sorry I have hurt you. Please know I am safe and happy like never before. Everyone I know and love is here except you, but you will see me again. Until then, I will be with you always, just not the way you knew me. You will be okay, Mom. Work through the grief and be gentle with yourself. Someday you will laugh again. I was not meant to grow old. It was my time. I did struggle with life. So many things (accidents) happened to me, and this was the biggest thing. Maybe it saved me from something worse down the road. I am safe. I am happy. I am loved. You will be okay. All my love.

Your son,

Lee

Wednesday, March 7

A second night of little sleep. My brain won't shut off. Questions and thoughts bombard me. Were you scared when you died? I hope not. I hope you saw everyone you knew and felt welcomed. I know I will survive this, but right now, the pain is beyond anything I've ever known. You could hack off my arm, and it couldn't hurt more. The child I birthed, nurtured, loved, and cherished has been ripped from me. I won't stop these tears. I need them to cleanse my soul. I will let them come when they need to.

Love, Mom

Thursday, March 8 (3 a.m.)

Dear Lee,

Awake for most of the night again. I picture the pile of empty coal bags thrown in the corner of your garage. You opened a bag, shoved the coal in, and tossed the bag aside. Repeat. Repeat. Repeat. I feel the anger seep up through my sadness. I wonder if I will ever be free of the grip of grief? Will I have to don a mask forever for the outside world? I grieve for you, and I grieve for me. At least you got the better end of the deal.

Love, Mom

Sunday, March 11

Dear Lee,

A professional looked at your coal furnace today. He asked if there had been a tragedy. Dad said, "Yes," but said no more. He said it was an accident waiting to happen. Dad is suffering from so much guilt. He thinks this is all on him. Please let him know it's not his fault.

Love, Mom

Monday, March 12

Dear Lee,

I found something you wrote when I turned sixty. You said we liked to eat and play board games together. You said you were looking forward to us playing the Game of Thrones game together. We never got to play.

Love, Mom

Tuesday, March 13

Dear Lee,

I hate Tuesdays.

Love, Mom

Wednesday, March 14

Dear Lee,

I feel a sense of calm today. A moment of respite from the sadness. Are you trying to let me know, all is well? I hope you are happy and wouldn't want to come back if given the chance. If you are happy, then I will bear this pain.

Love, Mom

Thursday, March 15

Dear Lee,

Another sleepless night. I cry silent tears, so I don't wake Dad, who probably is awake, too. I can already feel today is going to be a rough day. All I can do is hang on and ride it out.

Love, Mom

Wednesday, March 21

Dear Lee,

I try to distract myself with shows, but the pain has found me again, squeezing my chest and head. I'm so tired. Grief is exhausting. I don't think I should avoid the pain. I think it's better to face it. I try to imagine what you would say to me right now. Would you apologize? Hug me? Tell me you are happier now than ever before? I wish you would tell me.

Love, Mom

Friday, March 23

Dear Lee,

Dad and I are going away for the weekend. At least no one will know me.

Love, Mom

Saturday, March 24

Dear Lee,

It's cold, but the lake is beautiful. We went to the pool and the hot tub, then out to dinner. It felt good to do something normal.

Love, Mom

Sunday, March 25

Dear Lee,

I feel okay today. I think, "Maybe I will survive this." When I got home, there was a heart-shaped locket April left for me. I will put a small lock of your baby hair in there, along with your picture.

Love, Mom

Monday, March 26

Dear Lee,

Jay went to Seattle for business, and the first person he met was named Lee. Coincidence? I don't think so.

I was given a beautiful painting of us together from a friend. It touched my heart. I will hang it in the bedroom and say good morning and goodnight every day.

Love, Mom

Tuesday, March 27

Dear Lee,

I dreamed of when we picked out Ruby together (our family Beagle). You picked her because you shared a birthday. You held her tight all the way home rubbing her soft ears. I'm sorry you didn't get to say goodbye when we put her down. I imagine her with you and Buddy now.

Love, Mom

Wednesday, March 28

Dear Lee,

Someone asked if I was excited to retire. Excited? My son is dead. My world had crumbled and imploded, and you think I might be excited? No one understands what I feel. Will I ever be excited again?

Love, Mom

Thursday, March 29

Dear Lee,

My last day at work. I turned off my office light, closed and locked the door, and ended a twenty-one-year career. No party. No celebration. I'm home alone crying instead. I'm not sure what to do now or where this road will lead me, but I'm forced to travel it. I know the path will be rough. I just hope I don't lose my way. I need a guiding hand, and I hope it's yours.

Love, Mom

April 2018

Sunday, April 1

Dear Lee,

Today is Easter. You should be walking through the door for breakfast or dinner. This is the first holiday without you. I cannot go to church today and maybe never again. Jesus rose, and now you are celebrating Easter with him. I hope it's festive.

Love, Mom

Monday, April 2

Dear Lee,

Today is the first full week of retirement. I'm scared.

Love, Mom

Tuesday, April 3

Dear Lee,

Ernie told me to slow down, be quiet, reflect, and you will come to me. He said to talk to you. Does he mean out loud?

Love, Mom

Wednesday, April 4

Dear Lee,

An inspector looked at your furnace today and determined the furnace was outdated, but not faulty. We wanted to make it someone else's fault, but it looks like the blame falls on you. Dad still feels guilty. I hope he can forgive himself. It's not his fault.

Love, Mom

Thursday, April 5

Dear Lee,

I've read there are no accidents. Wasn't your death an accident? I'm confused.

Love, Mom

Friday, April 6

Dear Lee,

Ernie gave me a book to read called, *We Don't Die,* by George Anderson, who says death is not the end of life, but a beginning or continuation. This gives me hope. I was taught about Heaven, but you either got in, or you didn't. Or you rested in peace until Judgement Day. I will open myself up to these ideas, pray more, and seek the truth. I think my grief journey will send me down a more spiritual path.

Love, Mom

Saturday, April 7

Dear Lee,

I watched a video of you dancing at a wedding. You were so full of life. And it confirmed what a good dancer you are. I hope you are still dancing.

Love, Mom

Sunday, April 8

Dear Lee,

As I put some apples in the refrigerator, I remembered you liked your apples cold rather than room temperature. I'm so afraid little memories like these will fade.

Love, Mom

Tuesday, April 10

Dear Lee,

I had my first reiki healing tonight. Thank you for coming through. She said you were an old soul not meant to live to old age, and I knew deep in my soul but pushed it down. I thought of the shower before you were born. Maybe my soul "knew." She said you were playful and didn't like the confines of being an adult. True. You showed her Monopoly money, and it made me smile. You always wanted to play Monopoly on our game nights. The rest of us would groan, but we would play. You usually won, and Anna often quit. She also said my angels are keeping me safe. I have been so scatterbrained, so I am grateful they are watching over me. She saw Buddy with you. I know it's Buddy because she said he stood watch over you until we found you. I am forever grateful to the little neurotic dog. I'm glad he is by your side. "Look for hearts" was the last thing she told me. I felt like I had a connection with you for the first time.

Love, Mom

Wednesday, April 11

Dear Lee,

The comfort from last night has carried over into today. I think about the ways you could have passed and try to be grateful you simply fell asleep, and your soul left quickly, quietly and painlessly. I imagine you being greeted by your grandparents and many relatives, who embraced you in a loving group hug. If this truly is where you are meant to be, then I will try to focus on what you have gained rather than what I have lost. I do believe life does not end. We only shed our bodies.

Was it you I just felt? A tingle or little brush across the back of my neck. I hope so.

I met my friend for lunch today, and she brought me a gift, in a little bag, with hearts on it. Thanks for the sign.

Love, Mom

Saturday, April 14

Dear Lee,

I wondered what to do with the hundred-plus tee shirts you owned. They are just too personal to discard or give away. I was told someone wants to make a quilt for me. What a beautiful gesture, but it's just too much to comprehend right now, so I say I'll think about it.

Love, Mom

Wednesday, April 16

Dear Lee,

Alex (Lee's cousin) asked me if I'm okay with him naming his baby after you. The baby is due in July. His name will be Samuel Lee. I hope he's a redhead.

Love, Mom

Tuesday, April 17

Dear Lee,

When I drove by the house where you spent the first two years of your life, it felt like every memory flashed through me in an instant.

Love, Mom

Thursday, April 19

Dear Lee,

Anna's co-workers donated sixty carbon monoxide detectors to the Health Department today. Lives will be saved. Just not yours.

Love, Mom

Tuesday, April 24

Dear Lee,

Ernie warned me the lowest point comes around four months. I think it's here. The crushing feeling is back. I feel it in my throat, making it hard to swallow or even breathe. I alternate between extreme sadness and intense anger. I was at your house and yelled at you for the terrible pain and mess you left us with.

Love, Mom

Wednesday, April 25

Dear Lee,

Ernie says to get in and get out, but today I'm in, and I don't know how to get out. I feel like I am being smothered in a bog. The spiral down is like madness. Death would be preferable. How could you have left me? How could you have hurt me so much? And sure, you're okay. You're happy, safe, wonderful, and *having the time of your life.* What about my shattered heart? Didn't you know what this would do to me? Didn't God know what it would do to me? Stretch me? Make me a better person? I don't want to be a better person. I just want you. I was happy. What will I be now? Who will I be?

BROKEN AND SMASHED.

I hug your picture, and I think how you cried when I would sing "You Are My Sunshine." Now I cry as I pretend you sing to me.

"You are my sunshine, my only sunshine. You make me happy when skies are gray. You never know dear, how much I love you. Please don't take my sunshine away. The other night dear, as I lay sleeping, I dreamt I held you in my arms. As I awoke, dear, I was mistaken, so I hung my head, and I cried."

I miss you so much.

Love, Mom

Thursday, April 26

Dear Lee,

I smelled rotten eggs in your house for two weeks before you passed when I took care of Buddy. I told Dad I was glad we didn't have a coal furnace because it was so stinky, but I never mentioned it smelled like rotten eggs. I didn't know it indicated a problem with the furnace. How long was the poison building up? If only I had known. Could I have saved you? Now I understand guilt.

Love, Mom

Friday, April 27

Dear Lee,

I discovered a Facebook group tonight called Helping Parents Heal. I tried some other groups, but they didn't feel right. This group helps bereaved parents become "Shining Light Parents." I'm not sure what it means, but this group feels right to me. Maybe you helped me find them.

Love, Mom

Saturday, April 28

Dear Lee,

Do you like how you live now? No responsibilities. I wonder what you do. What is your new role? Are you teaching gaming? I picture you under a pile of kids like you would be with your nephew and nieces. Do you tell them stories? Make them laugh? Show them your monkey face?

Love, Mom

May 2018

Tuesday, May 1

Dear Lee,

I'm going to Ernie's group tonight. I need to see people can come back to life after losing a child.

I didn't like the group, or maybe it's too soon. A woman sat next to me and held my hand. I was grateful because I felt so alone and lost.

Love, Mom

Wednesday, May 2

Dear Lee,

I learned about using meditation to connect with your loved one. I will try this, and maybe through practice, it will happen.

Your work clothes went to a program to help men entering the work world. You donated three suits, sixteen pairs of pants, twenty long-sleeve, button-down shirts, and six polos. It was hard to let go of your things, but they are just things, and I know you would want to help people. I kept the tee shirts and ties.

Love, Mom

Thursday, May 3

Dear Lee,

I asked for a sign and then spotted a heart-shaped cloud while sitting outside. Thank you. I love you and miss you so. I selfishly want you here. I have so many questions. Is it true there are no accidents in the world? A person fulfills their purpose and moves on to a higher one? As I look at the heart cloud, your words come to me, and I write:

Dear Mom,

Here is the sign of my love, which is with you all the time. Carry it with you and let it wipe away your tears. I am sorry I had to leave, but you know in your heart, I am well. There is so much I can do now with no hindrance. I am happy and want you to be happy too. I will wait for you, and once you are here, you will understand. Be still, listen, and feel my presence. Use mediums to communicate until you learn how to do it yourself. I am with you always.

I love you,

Lee

Love, Mom

Saturday, May 5

Dear Lee,

Last night I got drunk. Grieving is hard enough without throwing alcohol into the mix. I ranted and raved, but it's out of me now. Sitting at my sister's house, I look at the backyard and picture you and your cousins playing. Good memories. Hard memories. Note to self: spirits plus spirits don't mix.

Love, Mom

Sunday, May 6

Dear Lee,

I tried a guided meditation, and while comforting, I'm not sure I saw you or just imagined it. Maybe it doesn't matter. I was happy to be in a place of such beauty and walk with you. Both grandparents walked arm in arm on either side of you while we held hands. Then we sat on a stone bench, under a tree, by a river. I will continue to explore this.

Love, Mom

Monday, May 7

Dear Lee,

I forgive you for being careless. You made a mistake. Unfortunately, it was fatal.

Love, Mom

Tuesday, May 8

Dear Lee,

I have always struggled with my faith. I spouted the Catechism, but I didn't feel a real connection. I hope you aren't the price to find faith because it's too high. I don't think it works like that. But I do think there is a lesson here and an opportunity for growth. I accept the challenge. What choice do I have?

Love, Mom

Wednesday, May 9

Dear Lee,

I don't fit in anymore. I'm no longer normal.

Love, Mom

Friday, May 11

Dear Lee,

Seven years ago, today, Grandpa died. It's hard losing a parent, but there's no comparison to losing a child.

Love, Mom

Sunday, May 13

Dear Lee,

This is the first Mother's Day of how many without you?

Love, Mom

Monday, May 14

Dear Lee,

Ernie is now gone too. I knew I wouldn't have him for long, but I needed him longer. I feel abandoned. My heart is so heavy. I hope I can do this without him.

Love, Mom

Tuesday, May 15

Dear Lee,

I tried Ernie's grief group again. It was awful. Many of them have been going for years. They seemed so sad. I thought, "Is this how I have to be for the rest of my life?" They encouraged me to keep coming, but I'm not going back.

Love, Mom

Wednesday, May 16

Dear Lee,

I can't sleep, so I prayed to God to bathe me in strength, peace, and love. I imagined being filled up with a bright light hoping it will break up the unbearable heaviness of sorrow and pain.

Love, Mom

Thursday, May 17

Dear Lee,

Today I want to die. I understand why parents choose to follow their children. I'm glad Dad is at work, so he doesn't see how low I am. I cannot do anything. I sit here and stare. How am I not dehydrated from crying all these tears? I'm going back to bed until Dad gets home. Then I will pretend I'm doing okay.

Love, Mom

Friday, May 18

Dear Lee,

I saw three redheads today. What are the chances? Was this a sign? Did I see three redheads for a reason? I hope. I will try to believe.

Love, Mom

Saturday, May 19

Dear Lee,

Grandma died twenty years ago today. She was only sixty-nine. Maybe I will get lucky and check out early, too. I used to be happy. Loved life. Now I dread the years ahead.

Love, Mom

Sunday, May 20

Dear Lee,

Somehow this pain and sadness have become familiar, even comfortable. How could this be? Could this be an enjoyable state to be in? Do I want people to feel sorry for me? I'm told I will survive this pain. I will live again. Love. Laugh. Enjoy life. I hope.

Love, Mom

Monday, May 21

Dear Lee,

Surprising how I can have a semi-normal day. Of course, I think of you every waking moment, but I'm not crying so much today.

I noticed the record player we got for Christmas. It's dusty and forgotten in a corner. Will I ever play music and dance again?

Love, Mom

Tuesday, May 22

Dear Lee,

Thank you for coming to my dream. It was fleeting, but you were so beautiful. About two years old. You were the sweetest boy. So sensitive.

Love, Mom

Wednesday, May 23

Dear Lee,

I wish you could tell me why this happened. I had such a good life. I was happy. I was proud of my kids. Was I too proud? Is this why? Did I have to be humbled? Why do I need to suffer this pain? Why does any mother have to suffer like this? Will I have to pretend for the rest of my life? Smile, laugh, joke while crying and screaming on the inside? How am I going to survive? Are you with me? Please let me know. Brush the tears off my face. Sit beside me. Be with me for just a moment, so I can breathe again. This is too hard.

Love, Mom

Thursday, May 24

Dear Lee,

I hate the news. So much bad news. So many people are hating and hurting each other. Why? Your death was an accident. You made a mistake, and it was a fatal one. Maybe it would be different if someone had caused your death. At least I would have someone to be angry at. Maybe if I was angry, I wouldn't be so sad. No, I would probably be angry and sad.

I WISH:

You were here.

You had changed the furnace when you bought the house.

Dad had asked you how it worked and how to clean it.

I had mentioned the rotten egg smell.

I knew you were in trouble.

I could hear your voice.

I had talked to you more rather than text.

I had dinner at your house just one time.

I had a note or letter from you.

I could go on and on with wishes, but it wouldn't change a thing. Maybe I can change my wishes into hopes.

Love, Mom

Sunday, May 27

Dear Lee,

I am learning so many things about the afterlife from Helping Parents Heal. This group is helping me, maybe even saving me. I learned about soul planning, but I'm not sure how I feel about this. Why would I agree to such a thing? Is this why I cried in the shower before you were born? Did I know you were going to leave before me? What is the reason?

Love, Mom

Monday, May 28

Dear Lee,

I read grief has the power to transform us. It may be too soon, but I have to do something with all this pain. I hope I can learn to manage this grief and someday make a difference. What will I do to help others? Please help me figure this out.

Love, Mom

Tuesday, May 29

Dear Lee,

I am determined to learn as much as I can to connect with you. I listened to a medium who said your loved ones direct you to the right medium. Help me find the right medium. I need to hear from you.

Another load to the mission today. So tough. As I drove home, two butterflies went past my windshield. Then another as I pulled into the driveway. I'm not sure if I feel better, but I'm glad you are with me.

Love, Mom

Thursday, May 31

Dear Lee,

I had a phone reading with Troy Griffen, who I found through Helping Parents Heal. He knew it was a sudden, unexpected death. He saw you playing Hot Wheels with kids. He said you were like a big kid yourself. You smirked and told him I had skipped more than one chapter in my book. Did you expect me to tell you all the bad things I did? You said I will help others and you will be with me. Troy said you wanted me to make something you loved for your birthday. It could only be clam chowder. I was never going to make it again, but since you requested it, I will. I was shocked when Troy said I was wearing a locket, connected to you, and I hold it a lot. I was holding it at that moment. You told me to take it off and put it in a sacred place, as it wasn't doing me any good. Thank you for connecting with me. I feel better. This has to be real.

Love, Mom

June 2018

Friday, June 1

Dear Lee,

I now understand how precious and fragile life is, a lesson I learned hard and fast. I wish I hadn't.

Love, Mom

Saturday, June 2

Dear Lee,

You must approve of the new RV Dad and I bought because I found a dime right after we bought it. Then Dad stopped for gas and saw a dragonfly, on the door. It rode all the way home on there. I hope you will ride along with us.

Love, Mom

Sunday, June 3

Dear Lee,

I'm trying to accept this new reality of your existence, but it's hard. I know you are enjoying your evolved state. You loved all things concerning space, time, and things ethereal, and now you are part of it. "I'm having the time of my life," you said.

Love, Mom

Tuesday, June 4

Dear Lee,

I no longer believe in coincidences. I had lunch with Mario's mom. (Lee and Mario went to school together. Mario was murdered in 2016.) I like to think you both were with us. But what happened when we finished lunch was no doubt orchestrated by Ernie. Our waitress was the same one Ernie introduced me to the one time we had lunch there. She does not normally work on Tuesdays, yet she was there. I introduced her to Mirella then spotted a young woman from Ernie's group who did not know either woman. So, I am beginning to understand how Spirit works. Thanks for the lesson, Ernie.

Love, Mom

Wednesday, June 5

Dear Lee,

If you are well and happy, I will try to accept the new reality of your existence. (I felt warmth and a pressing on my back which I believe was Lee hugging me.) You know this is a long, difficult journey, so keep on helping and hugging me. I love you so much. I will try to be open to your signs.

Love, Mom

Friday, June 8

Dear Lee,

I try not to count, but my brain screams; it's been five months. The pain is acute and physical right now. I am having a hard time eating, so I made a smoothie, hoping to get it down. I just want to curl up in a ball and wait for a better day.

Love, Mom

Saturday, June 9

Dear Lee,

It's my birthday. I found out my friend's son has been missing for nine weeks. The police think he was murdered. I feel a moment of relief and gratitude because you simply fell asleep and moved out of your body—no terror or pain.

Love, Mom

Monday, June 11

Dear Lee,

I try to pretend I'm okay, but when people are talking and laughing around me, I want to scream, "My son is dead. Why are you carrying on like nothing has happened?" Then I realize, nothing has happened in their world so they can't possibly understand the broken, shattered woman, I am. I pray, you never know.

Love, Mom

Wednesday, June 13

Dear Lee,

I'm trying to learn as much as I can about the afterlife, consciousness, and God. I'm listening to podcasts and reading books, trying to absorb what has happened and where you are. Trying to figure out why this has happened is pointless anyway.

Love, Mom

Friday, June 15

Dear Lee,

There's a long line at the Salvation Army Emergency Services. I feel so privileged. I wish I could go down the line and hand money to each person. No matter what, they are human beings, and we should help them.

Love, Mom

Wednesday, June 20

Dear Lee,

This morning is the most peace I have felt so far. I am beginning to understand your soul came here, to be Lee, for your time. I still wrestle with whether your death was planned or simply an accident, but in the end, it doesn't matter or change things. It's 5:30 a.m., and I look up at the sky of pinks and blues, changing rapidly. And I know God is good and has made this for us to enjoy. I hope I can learn the lessons of love: caring, kindness, and purpose. There is one brilliant stripe of color in the sky. It looks like the beginning of a rainbow. I will take it as a sign.

Love, Mom

Thursday, June 21

Dear Lee,

Aunt Kathy and I are on our way to Florida. I think of all the vacations you will never have, and I start to sink. Then I hear, "But I'm on the best vacation. Paradise." Then I feel you making your monkey face at me, and I smile.

Love, Mom

Friday, June 22

Dear Lee,

When a cardinal landed on the fence, Aunt Kathy said she liked red-headed woodpeckers better. No sooner did she say it, and one landed on the tree. I don't know how this all works, but the signs are so uplifting.

Love, Mom

Sunday, June 24

Dear Lee,

Thank you for the sign tonight. I look down at dinner, and there's a dime near my foot.

Love, Mom

Tuesday, June 26

Dear Lee,

I think about how careless people are with their lives. Carelessness can cost you your life. You were careless, and you paid with your life. Carelessness cost me the gift of you. I will say a prayer for the careless people to wake up and treasure life before it slips away from them.

Love, Mom

July 2018

Sunday, July 1

Dear Lee,

Thank you for the incredible sign you gave to Dad while I was away. He wants to believe in the afterlife, but he has doubts.

This is how it happened:

Tom was sitting outside in front of the garage about 9:30 p.m. when he heard a rattle inside the garage. He went to investigate and felt and heard a cold whoosh go past him. He said, "Is that you, Lee?" He continued to talk and waited for a long time, but nothing else happened. Then he spotted something red in the rafters he had never noticed before. He climbed up and found a little red, Hot Wheels car. He turned it over, and it had 1987, on the underside, the year Lee was born. What Tom did not know was that Troy Griffen said Lee was playing Hot Wheels with kids.

I have been feeling brushes and tingles lately like bugs are crawling on me. Is this you? I also hear you responding in my head. I'm sure it's you.

Love, Mom

Monday, July 2

Dear Lee,

I learned about spirit guides. I didn't know we had one from birth to death, but I like it. We have one whether we know it or not. It sounds like a thankless job to me. I learned to imagine a whiteboard, and the first name to pop up is your guide. Mine is Harriet. I have so much to learn.

Love, Mom

Tuesday, July 3

Dear Lee,

Sometimes I pretend you moved away, and I will see you soon. I know it's silly, but sometimes the pain is unbearable, so I pretend.

Love, Mom

Wednesday, July 4

Dear Lee,

Samuel Lee was born on Monday. I think he's going to be a redhead.

Love, Mom

Thursday, July 5

Dear Lee,

A two-year-old drowned. I know the pain the parents are feeling. I wish I could help them. I will send them love from my heart. Grief is so hard. I wish I could take it from them. I pray no one in my family ever experiences this level of pain. Please God spare them ever knowing.

Love, Mom

Friday, July 6

Dear Lee,

I did a guided meditation tonight, and it helped to lift some sadness. My heart is splayed open, but I feel something germinating in there. I know I have to work hard to not let grief control me for the rest of my life. Please guide me to a greater understanding. I hope I can learn love and grow in a new way.

Love, Mom

Sunday, July 8

Dear Lee,

Dad and I are at Lily Dale. There is so much peace here.

Love, Mom

Monday, July 9

Dear Lee,

I went to a healing service today. I knew I would cry, but after, I ran out with tears streaming down my face, which turned into explosive sobs. It felt like I was spewing poison. A young woman approached me and asked if I was okay. I said, "No. I lost my son in January." And I immediately heard, "But Mom, I'm not lost. I'm right here." The young woman hugged me, and I thanked her for her kindness. Then I sat for a long time to reflect.

Love, Mom

Wednesday, July 11

Dear Lee,

In *Your Soul's Plan* by Robert Schwartz, he says we plan our lives before we come here to learn lessons. I don't think I believe this. Why would I agree to have you die before me? What would be the lesson? But true or not, I would do it all again, even if I knew the outcome. All thirty years. All of it. The good and the bad. I would soak up every little bit of it, like a treasure. Because I know how precious and fragile life is.

Love, Mom

Thursday, July 12

Dear Lee,

I found a heart-shaped wine spill on the balcony table where we are staying. It made my heart flutter. I showed it to Dad and told him it was his birthday gift from you.

Love, Mom

Friday, July 13

Dear Lee,

I still can't wrap my head around soul plans, but as I reflect on your life, I think about all the ways you were different and the hard things you went through and wondered if somehow it was a plan. I will continue to learn about this.

Love, Mom

Saturday, July 14

Dear Lee,

Jay told me when you moved into your house, you said, "I'm going to die in this house." He assumed you meant you were never going to move again, but it's a strange way to put it. I wonder if there was something more to it? Why would you put it that way? Did you have an inkling? Was it coming from your soul?

Love, Mom

Tuesday, July 17

Dear Lee,

Were you messing with my phone? I was listening to the reading I had, at Lily Dale, when suddenly it switched to a guided meditation. I go back to the reading, and it switches to a song. When it happened a third time, it made me laugh out loud. It was you, wasn't it?

Love, Mom

Wednesday, July 18

Dear Lee,

Last fall, you told me you were the happiest you had been in a long time. Was it a signal you had completed your journey on earth? Then I had my dream. Did you have a premonition too? Maybe this is all part of a plan. I am trying my best to understand all of this, but acceptance will be much harder. The pieces seem to be falling into place.

Love, Mom

Thursday, July 19

Dear Lee,

I struggle. I try my best, but I struggle. I am broken. I meditate, pray, and read. But this road is hard. I know you are fine and having the time of your life. I hope it's enough to see me through.

Love, Mom

Saturday, July 21

Dear Lee,

I rejected the idea of reincarnation, in the past, but now I'm reconsidering the idea. Have we shared a lifetime before this one? Will we again? I don't want to come back if I have to lose a child again. It's much too hard, even if there is an important lesson to it.

Love, Mom

Monday, July 23

Dear Lee,

Your car crapped out on Anna today, and I heard, "I'm so glad I don't have to deal with that BS anymore. I'm having such a great time here." Lucky you.

Love, Mom

Tuesday, July 24

Dear Lee,

I had an energy healing tonight. Melanie said, "Wow, oh wow," as she waved her hands over my chest. She said she felt deep loss and sadness. My tears flowed. Then you dropped in.

There were many validations, but a few stood out.

- You passed from a weird accident.
- You liked the idea of your picture on the grave marker. (We hadn't told anyone that.)
- There would be three to five words on it. It ended up six. (Son, Brother, Nephew, Uncle, Cousin, Friend)

- You showed her your blue and gold basketball sneakers from ninth grade.
- You showed her your dark green sweater and your box of trinkets.
- She saw a one, two, or a twelve. This did not mean anything to me. I couldn't figure it out, so she said to take it with me.

I left the session feeling somewhat lighter. I know it won't last, but I'm thankful for a little reprieve.

Love, Mom

Wednesday, July 25

Dear Lee,

I still feel the positive effects of the healing. How long will it last? I have had five readings since you passed. Most have said you are like a big kid, playing with kids. I am picturing this and decide to get the little Hot Wheels car that Dad found, to put it by your picture. When I picked it up, it felt like a lightning bolt hit me—car 12. I started laughing, and tingles exploded on the left side of my head, which I now recognize as you. I feel like a door has kicked open to something spiritual, which can't be closed.

Love, Mom

Thursday, July 26

Dear Lee,

I opened up your box of trinkets. It's the blue art box you got for Christmas when you were a little boy. It's full of movie stubs, concert tickets, licenses, a learner's permit, pins, a yoyo, photos, and a whoopee cushion. I didn't realize how sentimental you were, like you treasured every memory, as if deep in your soul, you knew your life would be short.

Love, Mom

Sunday, July 29

Dear Lee,

Brushes and tingles woke me at 3:30 a.m. Are you letting me know that you were with us last night when we met your college buddies? I have to believe this because to not believe would be un-bearable.

Love, Mom

Monday, July 30

Dear Lee,

You have a doppelganger! Uncle Tim and Aunt Gina are traveling with friends in California. Their friends chose a brewery for lunch, and as they walked in, there on the wall was a picture of someone who looks just like you. Uncle Tim said it took his breath away. He called me and asked if you were ever in California because he was so sure it was you. I told him that you had not. He sent me the picture, and I was stunned. He is the spitting image of you. Out of all the breweries in Paso Robles, why did they pick this one to stop at? I'm beginning to see how this all works and it's amazing.

Love, Mom

August 2018

Wednesday, August 1

Dear Lee,

I was arrogant and took everything for granted. I thought I was untouchable, but I was simply blind to the truth. I need to understand what life is all about and who I am. What did I come here to do and learn? What is my purpose?

Love, Mom

Thursday, August 2

Dear Lee,

Dad has Stage 2 Squamous Cell Carcinoma on his hand. It's not life-threatening as it was caught early, but I believe it was brought on by stress. He holds his feelings in.

Love, Mom

Friday, August 3

Dear Lee,

I can feel a slow transformation in me. In meditation, I asked for guidance as to what I am to do next. I understand I'm still early in grief, but I will do the work. I know I have a lot of tough firsts ahead, but I want to be a shining example for the family. My beliefs have changed. Your passing has washed away any doubt I had about the existence of God. I read a child's passing is for the parent's soul's progression. It's a high price, but I can't change it. I can only move forward. Ernie said you have two choices:

to get up or give up. I chose the first, for you, for me, for our family.

Love, Mom

Sunday, August 5

Dear Lee,

It's hard to socialize these days. The banter seems shallow and pointless. No one "gets it," and I wouldn't want them to, but it's easier to be with people who understand how I feel so I don't have to pretend.

I was floating, in a kayak, on Cayuga Lake feeling sad. I was alone, so I let my tears fall freely. I closed my eyes and asked for a sign, and when I opened them, I saw a butterfly. When I expressed my gratitude, I felt tingles on my head, and it elevated my mood.

Love, Mom

Monday, August 6

Dear Lee,

I joined another Facebook group, called Mediumship for the Grieving Heart. Do we discover, or are we led to these groups?

Love, Mom

Tuesday, August 7

Dear Lee,

I had a nightmare that Anna drowned. Please, God, don't let this be a premonition. I couldn't bear to go through this again. I just couldn't. Watch over your sister, Lee.

Love, Mom

Wednesday, August 8

Dear Lee,

I might write your story. I asked you to send a heart sign, by the end of the day, if I should do this. I probably shouldn't make demands for specific signs, but I did, and you came through. I had a feeling to look on a pile of dirt in our dug-up yard, and there was a big heart-shaped stone. I have a working title, *Lucky Lee*. Sometimes, I think you are lucky to be where you are: no worries, no problems, and having the time of your life. Sometimes, I wish I could trade places with you.

Love, Mom

Thursday, August 9

Dear Lee,

I was in a restaurant when Green Day's "Good Riddance" played. There's a line in it that says, "I hope you have the time of your life." It made me think of you. And I smiled.

Love, Mom

Friday, August 10

Dear Lee,

I am on a spiritual journey I never expected but now accept. It's hard to believe you left seven months ago. It's hard to believe I have survived this long, and yet I have. The groups, books, podcasts, radio shows, signs, and validations are helping me along this path. I look up at just the right moment and see a butterfly. I feel your brushes and tingles on the left side of my head. I hear you in my head. I doubted this at first but have learned not to, even at the risk of people thinking I'm crazy.

Love, Mom

Saturday, August 11

Dear Lee,

How do parents do grief without going down a spiritual path? I would be lost. This makes me grateful to everyone who has helped me along this difficult path so far.

Love, Mom

Sunday, August 12

Dear Lee,

I did a guided meditation. I invited Archangel Michael in and imagined him behind me, tall and formidable. Then I invited you in and felt a pressure on my back, and I knew you were with me. I immediately heard, "I'm okay." I asked you what you wanted me to know, and this is what I wrote:

I'm having the time of my life.

I'm with you.

I send many signs.

I love you.

I'm sorry.

You'll be okay.

Love everyone.

Then I felt a tingle on the top of my head. I will not doubt anything I think or feel.

Love, Mom

Tuesday, August 14

Dear Lee,

I miss your monkey face.

Love, Mom

Wednesday, August 15

Dear Lee,

Today I read your last text to me about the date you had set up. I cried hard, and you told me to delete it, but I'm not ready. I'll try not to read it, but I need it there. Then I heard you say, "Mim" in your funny voice (Lee's funny name for mom). I know you are with me, but I miss your physical presence. I know you hug me, but it's not the same. I'm trying. You know I'm trying.

Love, Mom

Saturday, August 18

Dear Lee,

I believe Dad met his spirit guide last night. He woke up and saw a form in front of the RV. It started coming toward the bedroom. He thought, "Oh, Lee, you've finally come." Then he saw a large, black man standing over him, who quickly disappeared. I'm happy he had this experience.

Love, Mom

Monday, August 20

Dear Lee,

Your headstone came in. I went to see it. It's so real and permanent, just like death.

Love, Mom

Tuesday, August 21

Dear Lee,

In meditation, I envisioned a beautiful garden. You sat across from me, and we talked. You reassured me you are fine. You said you know how difficult this journey is for me, but I am doing great, and you are proud of me. I told you I sometimes wish I was there with you because it's just too hard. You said the family needs me, and there's more for me to do. I want you to know I wouldn't harm myself. I would not hurt the family. Just like you promised me once, I now promise you.

Love, Mom

Friday, August 24

Dear Lee,

This morning's meditation was awesome. My parents, grandparents, cousins, and friends were there. I could sense many others around. I cried tears of connection and joy.

I bought two butterfly bushes for the cemetery and saw five butterflies afterward. The first one flew past my windshield right after the purchase. I spotted the second one as I was pumping gas. Then two more on our road and the final one at the cemetery. We plant tomorrow.

Love, Mom

Saturday, August 25

Dear Lee,

Dad and I planted the butterfly bushes. As I was digging, a butterfly showed up and landed on a bush. Then it took off and circled me several times before settling on the bush again. It then flew off. Anna stopped by and broke down crying. We finished up, and as we approached your car, a butterfly landed on the hood. Then it flew in the air and landed in front of her, where it flapped its wings for quite some time. I hope this will help her to believe you are alive and well. It pains me to see your siblings struggling, but thank you for the validations. And I look up in time to see two butterflies, as I write this.

Love, Mom

Tuesday, August 28

Dear Lee,

I woke up at 5:30 a.m. I love watching the day unfold. I marvel at the beauty of the sunrise. Do you marvel at this too?

Love, Mom

Wednesday, August 29

Dear Lee,

What would I give to have one more day, one more moment with you? Everything. I thought my life was good. I was happy and blessed, but I was blind. Now I see things differently. I have been forced to look inside, to re-evaluate my life and its path. I'd rather have you, but as long as I know you are with me, I can do this. I will heal and go wherever this path takes me.

Love, Mom

Thursday, August 30

Dear Lee,

I felt like I almost lifted out of my body during this morning's meditation. I imagined I was looking down on earth. It was beautiful and peaceful. I wanted to stay in meditation. We rush around, chasing material things. No wonder we have lost our spiritual way. I think about all the troubled souls in the world. I hope we can turn things around with faith, hope, and love. I want to do my part.

Love, Mom

Friday, August 31

Dear Lee,

Today is Jay's first birthday without you. This day will be hard for him. I hope you will send him a sign.

Love, Mom

September 2018

Sunday, September 2

Dear Lee,

The family got together today. I'm sure you were with us, but it was hard. It's difficult to be together and feel the gaping hole where you should be.

We went to the cemetery to see your headstone for the first time. I read something to the family then we released butterflies. It doesn't seem real, and yet it seems too real.

Today was harder than I thought. We gave your siblings the insurance money but instructed them not to open their envelopes until your birthday. I was afraid to see their faces.

Love, Mom

Tuesday, September 4

Dear Lee,

Your birthday is approaching, the first one with you in spirit. I don't want to, but I will make clam chowder, as I promised. Hummus too.

I met with a new healer today. Sara did some energy work, and you dropped in. She said I would have two breakdowns at the upcoming family wedding, and Dad would ask me to dance to a certain song. She also said she saw a golden thread from the top of my head, which stretches up to the Creator. I like this image. It comforts me. I pray that I open up to this.

Love, Mom

Wednesday, September 5

Dear Lee,

I know you want us to have fun at the wedding, but I don't even want to go.

Love, Mom

Thursday, September 6

Dear Lee,

We made it to Maryland. It's our first road trip with the RV. Did you ride along? The last thing I wanted to do was pile in a limo for a bachelorette party, but I did for my niece and sister. We went to the Power Plant in Baltimore, which is a blocked-off strip with several bars. Kathy and I were walking around and decided to sit down to listen to some live music. And in a dark corner, I spot a sign that says, "Lee's Tires." I don't know how this works, but your sign helped me get through the evening.

Love, Mom

Friday, September 7

Dear Lee,

Today is your thirty-first birthday and the first one without you. I wish you were here to celebrate like last year, but I could wish all day for the rest of my life, and it wouldn't change a thing. Maybe next year I will be able to celebrate you.

Love, Mom

Lee's 30th birthday

Sunday, September 9

Dear Lee,

The wedding was heavy, but we did the best we could. The men all wore your ties, which was a beautiful tribute to you. I had the two breakdowns, one in the church and the second during the reception. But the amazing thing was that Dad asked me to dance a slow dance. It was a country song, which was surprising since neither one of us are big country fans. Did you plant this idea in his head? I suspect this is how it works.

Love, Mom

Monday, September 10

Dear Lee,

So many Lee signs over the weekend. I saw a truck on the highway called Lee's Trucking. Then we passed Lee's Lane. And I noticed the name, Lee, on a mailbox. Thank you for getting my attention.

Love, Mom

Wednesday, September 12

Dear Lee,

Dad had the surgery on his hand for the cancer. Yes, he is fair and a redhead like you and had sixty years of sun exposure, but I believe that the cancer was brought out by stress. While we were waiting for the doctor, I sensed many beings in the room. This was a new experience for me. I sensed dad's spirit guide, angels, his parents, and you, of course. I felt someone had their hands over his head and another over his hand. And I knew the cancer would be gone. When we got to the car, Dad started crying. He said the doctor asked him how many kids he had, and he said four rather than five because he thought he would have a breakdown. He felt like he denied you. I told him that you understood.

I will always say I have five children.

Love, Mom

Thursday, September 13

Dear Lee,

I wonder if we might be soulmates. Have we spent other lifetimes together? I didn't believe in this before, but my mind is opening to the possibility.

Love, Mom

Sunday, September 16

Dear Lee,

Such a deep sadness has come over me the last few days, and I've been very teary. I guess that's how it will be from now on. Good days and bad days. The good days are those days I don't feel like I've been gutted, and there's a gigantic hole in me. But I know you are okay, and that's what is most important. I will take the pain and sadness as long as you are happy. That is all that matters to me.

It's hard to think we are entering the third season since you left. I think about you all the time—more than when you were here. I look at your picture, and sometimes even now, it doesn't seem real. I look at the door and imagine you walking through it. I look at a chair and pretend you are sitting in it with Buddy Velcro-ed to your side.

I'm on a path of spiritual discovery and development. I look at people differently now. I try not to judge. I know their souls came here to learn lessons. I know mine did too. I just wish mine wasn't so hard, but I can't change what is, so I will learn what I can and hopefully emerge as a new person full of love, compassion, and joy.

Love, Mom

Wednesday, September 19

Dear Lee,

I'm sitting out back watching hawks, butterflies, and leaves flying around. I realize more and more, there are no coincidences. I told Sara that my spirit guide's name is Harriet, and she said that last Friday, a Harriet came to her and kept bothering her while she was writing. She described Harriet as wearing an ethereal blue, a color connected to me. I saw her as a vibrant, zany spirit with white flowing hair. She said that Harriet had lived many lifetimes, which a spirit guide must do. Experience is everything. It is what we are here for. And though losing you, Lee, is not what I want, there must be a reason, a lesson, a quest I must go on now. And there's the question of a soul agreement. I struggle with that. If it's true we agreed you would leave this life before me, I wish I could take it back. I wish I could use my free will like a 'get out of jail free' card, but wishing is not reality. I'm stuck with what is. And maybe if I could change things, I would have to do this again in another life. So, I will try to find my path and accomplish what I can in this life. I will write our story when I am ready, with Harriet's guidance.

Love, Mom

Thursday, September 20

Dear Lee,

I'm grateful for Helping Parents Heal. I find so much comfort in this group. And I'm learning so much. I don't know where this will lead, but I don't have to know. I just need to follow and trust. I can't rush the process. It will unfold as it needs to. I am open to where I need to go and what I need to do. Thy will be done. I call upon my creator to help me accept the next step. I will focus on being a kind, compassionate, and loving person who neither harms nor judges. I understand now how my words and actions, both good and not so good, have impacted others. I will try to be mindful of that.

Love, Mom

Friday, September 21

Dear Lee,

I am fortunate to have five beautiful, healthy, and happy kids, one just happens to be on the spirit side of life. Maybe I can't see you, but I know you are with me. You tell me you are having the time of your life, and I believe you.

An unusual thing happened in the car today. I was reaching for something, in my purse, when the door locks clicked a few times. Then the flashers came on briefly. I did not touch anything as my right hand was in my purse, and my left on the steering wheel. Are you telling me to pay attention? You are right. Thank you.

Love, Mom

Saturday, September 22

Dear Lee,

I had seven losses in 2018. They all touched my life in some way, but none cut as deep as you.

Your house sold to a young couple. I hope they will be as happy and proud as you were to own your own home. Please watch over them.

Love, Mom

Sunday, September 23

Dear Lee,

I tried to watch a Buffalo Bills game, but it took me back to the game we went to in 2016. I know you were still struggling with Adderall. You had words with a guy, and I asked Dad to say something to you, and it turned into an ugly scene. We left. I heard you mutter, in the car, that maybe you would kill yourself and see how we liked that. I was so scared. I couldn't understand what was happening to you. I felt so helpless.

Love, Mom

Tuesday, September 25

Dear Lee,

I tried to go to a viewing today. Bad idea. I sobbed in the church, and I cried hysterically in my car.

Love, Mom

Wednesday, September 26

Dear Lee,

I try to imagine you on a wild adventure, on the other side. What have you seen? What have you done? Have you made new friends? Reconnected with old ones? Enjoyed family reunions? I think about you traveling the world seeing the sights. What experiences you must be having. It makes me wish I was seeing them too. But I know I can't. It's not my time. I know I have things to do. I will be patient. I know you here beside me. It's not what I want, but it's all I have now.

Love, Mom

Thursday, September 27

Dear Lee,

I had a powerful meditation this morning. I held your monkey shirt. You told me you are proud of me and how well I'm doing on this difficult journey. I thanked you and said, "I miss you." I started to get teary and heard you say I could wipe my tears, but not my nose on your shirt. You made me smile. I will work on this new relationship.

I grateful to be on this spiritual path, but the price is so high. I know you will help me guide me. I miss you and love you beyond words.

Love, Mom

Friday, September 28

Dear Lee,

A four-leaf clover popped into my head, an appropriate cover for a book with the title, *Lucky Lee*. Is this from my mind, or is this coming from you? Then I felt a mental poke from Harriet to go write.

During meditation, you told me Don would survive the lung cancer, which I felt was true in my gut. You said he would be a lesson to the family smokers, but there would be others. I asked, "Dad?" and you said, "Yes." I hope not. I can't take any more. Then I heard, "You can take it."

I want to bring everyone along this path. I want to shake them awake, but that's not how it works. I will be an example. I will speak my truth. Some might call me crazy or weird, but I can't let fear stop me from speaking what is growing in my heart.

Love, Mom

Sunday, September 30 (3 a.m.)

Dear Lee,

When you were a baby, I watched you. As you grew, I continued to watch you. Then you grew to be a man, and I still watched you. Now you watch me. I look at the stars, and I hear, "You are my Sunshine." I imagine you singing it to me. I felt tingling on my head. Then I heard, "You need sleep," but I had to write this down so I wouldn't forget. Thank you for this new connection. I will work on improving our relationship. I love you.

Love, Mom

Reading with Ann Van Orsdel:

- You and grandpa stepped in. Ann understood Grandpa passed by illness and said goodbye. You passed without an opportunity to say goodbye.
- She saw Dad and me with your body, but you didn't want to go back to the day (me neither). She said someone with a name that begins with a T called 911.
- Grandpa was the one to greet you. You didn't realize you had passed until you saw him, then you knew.
- You told Ann you wanted to take my pain away.
- Ann saw an S, and you told her it was a girlfriend, and you asked me to tell her you say hello and that you are okay. (This was a difficult task, but I honored it.)
- You showed her a blanket that would be made of shirts and said to put your name on it and use blue.

- You are happy Anna has your car, and there's something in the middle. (Anna said there's a French fry in there and she left it.)
- You showed Ann an L and said there's a young boy you have a bond with. Luke. You will come to him.
- You said I had a shift in my situation (I retired).
- You said you are learning from a professor in the family. (My cousin, Tony.)
- You showed a J (Jay) and said you have much love for him and a strong bond. And you love his girlfriend. She is a good support. You said Jay works hard and should watch for stress.
- Ann said I would write a book, and the title would be *Believe* or *Belief* or *Beyond Belief.* (He said he wanted it done by his first anniversary, but I was not able to.)
- You said I should meditate and do automatic writing, and you will download words and fragments. (He has kept his word on this.)
- You showed an F, a German spirit guide that will work with me. It's a long name, but I will shorten it. (I later came to know and name Fritz, who is my writing spirit guide. It's also the name of my Miniature Schnauzer that Lee brought to us.)

I asked if this was a soul plan, and Lee said, "No. It was an exit point, and you know that." He said the soul knows when to take it, and there was no trauma. He took it and hoped that he wasn't selfish.

You weren't.

Love, Mom

October 2018

Monday, October 1

Dear Lee,

Jay has been getting deer signs and thinks it's because of the cover story when he hit the guard rail. Thank you for sending such meaningful signs to your brother.

Love, Mom

Tuesday, October 2

Dear Lee,

What would be the price of never feeling this kind of pain, this grief? Never having known you? I would do it all over again, even knowing the outcome. What parent wouldn't give anything for a do-over or even five more minutes? I now know how precious life is, and not a moment should be wasted. You really know this when you've paid the highest price a parent can pay. But what you do with the pain matters. I don't know where this journey will take me, but I will set aside my doubts and fears and follow my path with trust.

Love, Mom

Wednesday, October 3

Dear Lee,

When I saw Grandpa's tree of life painting on the wall after meditation, I saw the cover of the book. Your story, our story. Then the title appeared, *beLEEve*, not *Lucky Lee*, as I had thought. Random thoughts started to surface.

- Break open the blockage of fear.
- Remember, with feeling.
- Trust that feeling.
- The story must be told.
- My soul knows what to do.

Love, Mom

Thursday, October 4

Dear Lee,

Passing through Lee, Massachusetts, I see a smiley face in the clouds, or is it your monkey face? Uncle Don will have surgery tomorrow to remove the tumor that has invaded his lung. I am sending out love and healing thoughts to my brother, and I ask God for a miracle because I don't think I could bear another loss this year. Is this selfish?

Love, Mom

Friday, October 5

Dear Lee,

While Don is in surgery, I think about your life. Was it a façade? Is everyone's life here just a façade? If the afterlife is our real home, then I think about how happy you must be, and it gives me some comfort. The tingles start, and *Oh the Places You'll Go* pops into my head. Are you telling me that you are loving your new experience, or am I making this up because I'm going crazy?

The surgery is taking too long. I know something is wrong. I feel it.

Don's outcome was not as favorable as we had hoped. The tumor was more invasive than the doctor thought. This will be a long and grueling recovery for Don. Please be with him.

Love, Mom

Saturday, October 6

Dear Lee,

In meditation, I ask if Don can bear the challenge he now faces. I hear, "This is his trial." Others will benefit and learn from it. There will be many lessons on many levels. What is my lesson from your death? What am I supposed to learn from all of this pain?

Love, Mom

Sunday, October 7

Dear Lee,

Where am I heading on this journey? What am I supposed to do? And I hear, "No fear. Fear blocks. Send fear away. Accept. Go inside. Let it come." So, I go inside, and love is there. God is there. You are there. Everyone is there. Everything is there. There is nothing but love. Love of self. Love of family. Love of life. Love of God. Love of everyone and everything. And it's been there all along. The price of this realization is high, but the lesson is real. I will find a way to honor this new understanding. And suddenly, I think of lemons—the yellow of the third chakra where wisdom and power reside. And I call upon the Holy Spirit to guide me.

Love, Mom

Monday, October 8

Dear Lee,

So many young people are exiting our world. I try to understand, but I can't. But I do understand how those parents feel. How can I help them? Can I help them? I want to, but how?

I go within and hear, "You will help many. Your heart will know the right time. Work on self. Prepare. Much to come. Look beyond for guidance. Hear them speak to you. Listen. Learn. Know. Believe. Trust. Set fear aside."

I wasn't expecting the mini reading in tonight's HPH meeting online, with over sixty people in attendance. Some of the evidence Jamie Clark brought forth:

- Jamie mentioned a painting of us together.
- There was a problem with your teeth (the college accident).
- Jamie saw 3-4 pictures of people together (you and two sets of grandparents on a table).
- You are with a male and a female with names that both begin with M (Mario and Margie?).
- You ride in the car with me and say you are a better driver.
- You touch me, and it feels like bugs crawling on me.

It's amazing that this can be done online. It gives me hope.

Love, Mom

Tuesday, October 9

Dear Lee,

98

It's awkward to be around people. Stay with me, Lee. I'm scared and lonely. And I miss my old life. I miss me. But mostly, I miss you.

I meditated outside. I felt so many tingles that I wanted to scratch, but I didn't because I knew it was you. I heard you in my head. "Keep going. Stay the path. Open. Believe. No fear. Study. Write. Stay the course. A beautiful, vibrant life awaits, full and wonderful. Avoid negative people and things." I opened my eyes and noticed an acorn on the patio. Acorns symbolize potential and strength. Thank you, Lee. I know it's for me. The message. The lesson. I accept. I will be strong. I will stay the course. I will learn and believe. I won't let fear, negative thoughts, or people put roadblocks before me. I can do this.

I beLEEve.

Love, Mom

Wednesday, October 10

Dear Lee,

As strong as I feel one day, the next comes crashing down, and I'm in the pits again. I go outside and sit with my eyes closed, listening to meditative music. When I open them, I see a butterfly, I watch it float away, and I send my sadness with it. Thank you for the sign. Thank you for the love and peace.

Love, Mom

Thursday, October 11

Dear Lee,

Who am I now? How will I put my broken pieces back together? What path do I follow? I have so many questions and feel so confused.

Love, Mom

Friday, October 12

Dear Lee,

It pains me to watch the family hurt so bad. I wish I could take it from them. I know Dad blames himself. I wonder if Jay will ever smile again? Todd and April have their families to concentrate on. I'm not sure if that is good or bad. It just is. Anna seems okay, but she is not one to share. I can hardly help myself, so I don't know what I can do for them. All I know is that it is so hard to be together with a giant hole in our midst. But we have to keep trying.

Love, Mom

Saturday, October 13

Dear Lee,

In meditation, I pictured you at the island in my kitchen, and I'm serving you clam chowder. Buddy was on your lap. It still hard to imagine this will never happen again. Even after all these months, it can still feel like a bad dream.

I want to ask friends and family to write letters with a memory of you that the family will read when everyone is ready. Do you think it's the right time to do this?

Love, Mom

Sunday, October 14

Dear Lee,

I spotted a small heart-shaped stone while hiking. I scratched your name on it and placed it on the rocks. I don't want anyone to forget you. You lived. You mattered.

Love, Mom

Monday, October 15

Dear Lee,

Today is my day of gratitude for you.

- I am grateful I had you for thirty years.
- I am grateful you didn't suffer.
- I am grateful you are happy.
- I am grateful you are having the time of your life.
- I am grateful you are with family and friends.
- I am grateful you are excited about all the new things you are learning.
- I am grateful you do not have the stresses and suffering of human existence.
- I am grateful you are with me now more than ever.
- I am grateful for your guidance.
- I am grateful for your love.
- I am grateful you work beside me.
- I am grateful you watch over your dad, siblings, nephew, and nieces.

Love, Mom

Tuesday, October 16

Dear Lee,

My grief rides with me. Sometimes it wears a seatbelt and behaves. And other times, the belt comes off, and it's unruly. Mostly my grief is colorless and odorless like the carbon monoxide that took your life. Not easily detected, but present nonetheless. Early on, my grief partnered with an addict who wanted to dull my pain. Not so much anymore though it sometimes tries to lure me to the dark side.

I can feel my grief shifting as I come to know it. I feel it change from that all-consuming raw pain to a chronic one you become used to and understand that it will always be with you. I will learn to live with grief, honor its presence, but I will not let it defeat me!

Love, Mom

Wednesday, October 17

Dear Lee,

Thank you for meeting me in meditation. I could feel the love. You said it's true that "Life here is fake, like a play." Real-life is on the other side. "There's so much to do here. It's unbelievable. If everyone knew, they would be dying to get here." (He laughs)

I feel like I'm in the middle of the murky waters of grief. I can see the light at the top, and I am working toward it. But I can still feel the pull, of the thick dredge, at the bottom. It's a constant battle, so I must be vigilant and do the work. As I was falling asleep, I felt something lift the hair, at my temple, as I looked at your picture, said goodnight and I love you.

Love, Mom

Thursday, October 18

Dear Lee,

I did a guided meditation this morning. I visualized being with you. Tears flowed, but from joy and peace. Then right in the middle of the meditation, I felt a jolt and wanted to scream, "No, I don't want this." I re-focused and settled back into the meditation. When I finished, I had a teary meltdown and thought, "How am I going to do this the rest of my life?" Instantly I heard, "Trust" and I settled back into the murky middle.

Love, Mom

Friday, October 19

Dear Lee,

I know about the baby. She didn't want to complicate your life. From her point of view, it was a selfless act, but I wonder how it affected you. I wish I could have that child because he is part of you, but I know he (I imagine a red-headed boy) is with you, happy and loved. And I love you both. I hope she loved you, too.

Love, Mom

Saturday, October 20

Dear Lee,

I'm having a hard day, so I remind myself about some truths.

- You are safe.
- You are happy.
- You are learning.

- You are having fun. (The time of your life, right?)
- You are with me.
- You love me more than ever.
- You send me signs.

I let this comfort me.

Love, Mom

Sunday, October 21

Dear Lee,

I'm thinking about starting a local Helping Parents Heal chapter. I know helping others will help me too. I decide to meditate on this, and before I can even formulate a question, I hear "Yes" in my head and the gentle squeeze, in my chest, when I know something is true. I'm not ready yet, but I will know when the time is right.

Love, Mom

Monday, October 22

Dear Lee,

I'm reflecting on the book, Ann said I would write. I can't have it done by your first anniversary. I'm scared. I don't know where to start or what to say. Somehow, I need to drive out the fear and dive in, but I'm not ready.

Love, Mom

Tuesday, October 23

Dear Lee,

Big trigger today. A Facebook video pops up of you wearing a mask while chasing the kids. Part of me is happy to watch you playing with them. You are so joyful and child-like yourself. Then I am sad because you will never play with them again. I asked for a sign, and when I look outside, I see at least ten mourning doves on the ground under the bird feeder. I've never seen so many at once. Their sound is sorrowful, but with a message of life, hope, and peace. Later, a butterfly flew across my windshield. Thank you.

Love, Mom

Wednesday, October 24

Dear Lee,

I met with Anne Warner to lay out the quilts. What a beautiful gesture. I am grateful for her kindness.

I had another mini-reading online tonight from Susanne Wilson during her Spiritual Explorers class.

The highlights were:

- You passed quickly. You just didn't wake up. Angels flew in and took you before your last breath.
- Susanne sees a guitar (Anna and Don).
- She mentions a painted, Kiss-like face. You say you look better than Gene Simmons. I have a picture of you dressed Kiss-like for Halloween.
- I look at your picture and say good morning and good night. Lee says this gives him bragging rights.

- You said, "I love you, Buddy," and she asks who Buddy is. I tell her about your dog. (Lee gave a touchdown sign for this.)
- Susanne says, you kiss my head. (The tingles prove it.)

Thank you for coming through. I know you don't like the limelight, so this was especially sweet.

Love, Mom

Thursday, October 25

Dear Lee,

I ask if you are ready for the road trip to North Carolina, and I hear, "Yep. I packed light." I sense you making your monkey face at me. Then George (Lee's best high school friend) pops into my head. Thank you, Lee. We will stop in Charlottesville.

A double rainbow appears as we near Charlottesville. I felt tingles all over my face and head, so I know you are with me, and this is the right thing to do. We spent time with George, and he was happy to see us. I was hoping for a sign, and maybe there was one. It's hard to pay attention with a lot going on. It's hard to be human.

Love, Mom

Sunday, October 28

Dear Lee,

My grief feels like a damp, heavy blanket today. Sad and uncomfortable, but not suffocating. I tried my best to put on a good face at the wedding.

Love, Mom

Tuesday, October 30

Dear Lee,

It's a 6 a.m. start for the ride home. As I near the car, I look down and there's a dime. Thank you. It's a long car ride, so lots of time to think. I need more understanding of what comes next, after this life, your life, where you exist now. I promise to work hard to understand and accept. (Tingles and a fluttery feeling.) I know you are guiding me, loving me, and supporting me, along with my angels, guides, and family. Thank you. I am filled with so much gratitude. The price of my awareness is high, and I would do anything to change it, but I can't, so I won't waste this opportunity to open and grow.

Love, Mom

Wednesday, October 31

Dear Lee,

Today my grief is calm. I feel some peace and acceptance. I feel a new beginning coming to me. I will make you proud. I will honor your life here, your life now, and our lifetimes together. Before bed, I looked at your picture like I do each night and said goodnight. I heard, "Goodnight, Mom." I said, "I love you," and heard, "I love you more." Then I said, "I miss you." When I didn't hear anything, I thought, "I got you there, didn't I?" But I know you miss me.

Love, Mom

November 2018

Thursday, November 1

Dear Lee,

Today is the best I have felt. I feel a lightness about me. I question how I could feel like this so soon. As I look at your picture, I smile and hear, "Just accept."

I had a wonderful reading with Isabella Johnson tonight.

- It was an unexpected passing. The manner was preventable, but not for you.
- Dad has guilt and needs to let it go. He can't fix everything.
- Lee tried to emulate Dad. He did his best to make him proud.
- My mom stood next to Lee with the soul baby.
- He acknowledged our donation of his clothes and detectors.
- He mentioned a family member with cancer. (Don)
- He flicks his dad on the head when he drinks too much.
- He talked about his girlfriend and said he was a "jackass," but he learned a lot and understood the part he played.
- Isabella asks why she sees the word "suffrage." I dressed as a Suffragette and marched in a parade, in 2017, to commemorate women winning the right to vote.

- Lee said he knew I was thinking about getting a tattoo. He said, "No tattoo, Mom." I said, "I do have free will."
- He said my spiritual awakening is his gift.
- He said, "Tell her I'm okay. I love you."

And the connection is over. I am grateful to Lee and Isabella for bringing us together tonight. I feel like there's a lifeline tethering us together, reassuring that you are with me. I heard, "I will always be with you," and felt tingles on my head. I need these validations as my belief strengthens, and hopefully, my ability to connect will too.

Love, Mom

Friday, November 2

Dear Lee,

The music I used for meditation this morning was incredible. I imagined Jesus surrounded by hundreds, maybe thousands of my family members all holding hands. Jesus was glowing. You were with my parents. The waters were swirling blue and purples. The sky was pink, orange, purple, and green. Then a brilliant, yellow sun rose, and majestic mountains appeared. I could hear seagulls and children. The music came to an end, and I was out of the meditation.

Tonight, I told Dad that you flick the side of his head (what you said in a reading) when he drinks too much. He admitted that he had felt something like a bug on his ear on two different occasions. "That's it," I told him. This is how this works, isn't it?

Love, Mom

Saturday, November 3

Dear Lee,

We were invited to All Soul's Day at church to commemorate the losses of 2018. It was dreadful. Dad was sobbing. I was angry. I couldn't even look at your siblings. I wanted to yell, "He's not dead." I don't feel like I belong there anymore. Maybe I never did. But I know for sure, I am done with organized religion.

Love, Mom

Sunday, November 4

Dear Lee,

I met your son in meditation this morning. He was maybe 6 or 7. He sat on my lap and put his arms around me. I saw him as a redhead just like you. I asked what his earth name would have been, and he said Nicholas Lee, but we would have called him Nickels. I felt such love for him and from him. I can't wait to meet him. I'm so sorry you had to suffer that pain. I wish I knew. I wish I had him. He is part of you. Now you are together.

I miss you so much. You reminded me that we have a closer relationship now, but I still would rather have you here in the physical.

Love, Mom

Monday, November 5

Dear Lee,

I wonder what I will do when my soul goes home? Jump off a mountain with you? Play with a tiger? Sit by a river?

Sing with the angels? Meet all the ancestors? Dress up in costume? March in a parade? Skate? Ride an elephant? Star in a play? Read a book? Write a book? I think about what you are doing all the time. I wish I could have a glimpse.

Love, Mom

Wednesday, November 7

Dear Lee,

During meditation, you remind me that it was our soul plan that you would leave first. It wasn't quite the time, but it was a perfect opportunity, so you took it. Is this how this works, or am I making this all up? Losing my mind? Lots of parents have lost kids. Why aren't they on this path? Why isn't this common knowledge? Then I hear, "They aren't ready for the truth." I ask, "Where is this truth leading me?" "Be patient. Let it unfold with time," is what I hear. I want to believe your passing was part of a plan, not just some random, senseless accident. Did you fulfill your purpose? What is the lesson for the rest of the family? Will they accept this idea? Will they believe? And I heard, "It's up to them. They will believe or not as it unfolds on their path. Place the truth before them, then step away."

Love, Mom

Thursday, November 8

Dear Lee,

I felt grandma's presence in meditation today. Tears fell, but I wasn't sad. She said she was my biggest cheerleader. I thanked her, and am so grateful for her support and love. I could have communicated with her all these years, but I wasn't ready.

Love, Mom

Friday, November 9

Dear Lee,

In meditation, I felt tingling and warmth all around me. I think it's time to start the book.

Love, Mom

Sunday, November 11

Dear Lee,

Yesterday I drank too much wine and let the mask slip. Today I am better. No poison. I need to feel this pain. It's the only way to heal. There's a benefit for Uncle Don today. He is so loved. His lung cancer is a kind of mini-death. Death of his old self to be renewed, by a painful ordeal. You can't go through life's painful trials and be your old self. You choose to be a better self or not. Whether it is losing a child or part of your lung, if you don't make something new and beautiful from it, what is the point? I hurt bad and always will, but I know I will have joy that lies right alongside the pain. They will mix in a sort of dance that will go on for the rest of my life. Thank you to all on your side who hold my heart tenderly and walk this path with me. I am grateful.

Love, Mom

Monday, November 12

Dear Lee,

Thank you for the signs today. I stopped for gas, and it came to $34, and I found a dime on the ground by the driver's door. Dad also had a sign today. He did a crossword lottery ticket, and only one word was completed. **LEE.**

Love, Mom

Wednesday, November 14

Dear Lee,

During meditation, I feel so many tingles all over my head and neck. These words come to me, and I write. "Death seems to strip you of all wants. Needs continue because they are necessary. There is nothing I want now. I have no desires. Where will this all lead?"

Love, Mom

Thursday, November 15

Dear Lee,

I feel so inadequate like I should be doing something, but I don't know what it is. And I hear, "The time will come when it is right. Feel, don't think." I guess I need to trust the process and let it unfold. I need to be sad, cry, and feel the grief.

Love, Mom

Friday, November 16

Dear Lee,

Dad was shoveling the walkway, at your house, when I heard, "Throw a snowball." This is not something I would normally do. I did it but missed him. Then I heard, "Lame," which made me smile. I then had an urge to make a snow angel. I wasn't going to, but I felt it came from you, so I did it. I hope an angel will watch over your house and the family who will live there after we sell it.

Love, Mom

Saturday, November 17

Dear Lee,

How can I let people know that life goes on? How do I tell them that you are alive and having the time of your life? It still hurts like hell but knowing this is the only way I have survived. If I didn't believe you were alive in a different form and time, and this human life was all there is, I couldn't do this life anymore. But I know you are proud of me for doing this hard grief work. I will come through this and carry this pain with me. I will help others who will suffer their loss.

Love, Mom

Sunday, November 18

Dear Lee,

Today is my mom's 90th birthday even though I know she looks 20, in the hereafter. I've learned that you can be any age you want. I know you didn't recognize her when you saw her until she showed herself older and sicker. Maybe Grandma will jump off a mountain to celebrate today.

I'm sitting here by the fire, thinking of how you will never walk through my door again, and I start to sink, so I stop myself. I need to replace these thoughts with happy ones, so I imagine you sitting right next to me wearing your green sweater. And I tell you how good it looks on you. Please sit with me and hold my hand.

Love, Mom

Monday, November 19

Dear Lee,

Dad continues to blame himself for not taking part in the care of your coal furnace. I tell him those thoughts serve no purpose because we can't change what is. But he is in a dark place today. He tries to hide it and doesn't cry in front of me, but I know. Today I have kind thoughts for Dad.

Love, Mom

Tuesday, November 20

Dear Lee,

Two days before Thanksgiving, the first one without you. And the first time I'm not making dinner for our family. We are going out to dinner. It will be strange. I ask for a sign. I'm usually not specific, but I ask for a rose. Then I log onto Facebook, and the first thing I see is a rose. Wow.

Love, Mom

Wednesday, November 21

Dear Lee,

It's the day before Thanksgiving. The sadness is creeping in, squeezing my chest. I need to let it happen, to give it time and attention, really feel it. I watch a video about grief and the holidays. I know Thanksgiving is just a day, but it's our family's favorite holiday, and the only time the extended family comes together. Right now, I would be cooking the second turkey for thirty to forty people. I feel so alone tonight. It's too quiet. No family around to celebrate with. My heart is heavy with quiet sadness. I dread tomorrow.

Love, Mom

Thursday, November 22

Dear Lee,

The flag football game was re-named in your honor. Jay couldn't go near the game, and my heart ached to see his pain. I tried to imagine you being part of the game or standing on the sideline with your arm around Dad, but I mostly felt numb. Dinner was weird but wasn't as awful as I thought it would be.

Love, Mom

Friday, November 23

Dear Lee,

Thank God yesterday is over.

Love, Mom

Saturday, November 24

Dear Lee,

Caitlin Johnson is naming her little girl after you. Her name will be Alanna Lee. I know you will watch out for this little girl.

Love, Mom

Monday, November 26

Dear Lee,

I am watching five turkeys in the yard. I look away, and when I look back, I only see four. This makes me feel sad.

Love, Mom

Wednesday, November 28

Dear Lee,

Can you go to other planets or even galaxies? I imagine you can, and this blows my mind. You are having the time of your life, aren't you?

Love, Mom

Thursday, November 29

Dear Lee,

I know you were with us on Thanksgiving, but I didn't feel your presence. I'm disappointed. Maybe I didn't pay enough attention. "I have the best of both worlds," you tell me.

In meditation, I hear, "Open your heart and push out the negative." I know you see me trying, and I know you are helping me along with many others from your side. I've got you all in my corner, so how can I fail? I will dig deep and trust.

Love, Mom

Friday, November 30

Dear Lee,

I have become a believer! I no longer fear death. There is no death. As a non-believer, I feared death. I know this now because I wanted to live to 100 years old. I thought it was because I was afraid of missing out, but I was afraid of what came next because I wasn't sure. I now understand that our fear of death is reflected in everything—our obsession with material things and youthful looks. I have released these things. I am free of them. I know when my time comes, I will say goodbye and go on to see what comes next.

Love, Mom

Saturday, November 31

Dear Lee,

As I drove up our road today, I pictured the time that you rode your Razor down the hill. And I hear in my head, "See, Mom, now I can't get hurt."

Love, Mom

December 2018

Sunday, December 2

Dear Lee,

I look at all the spots you would sit when you came over, and I wish I could see you there now. Maybe someday.

Love, Mom

Monday, December 3

Dear Lee,

I woke in the night and heard, "My life is rich and full. I'm incredibly happy. I don't miss out on any family stuff." This makes me happy.

Love, Mom

Tuesday, December 4

Dear Lee,

It was painful to see the Christmas tree at Todd's house. I pictured you and Luke playing the video game you played last Christmas. You were both laughing. There was so much joy then. Will I ever have a tree again?

Love, Mom

Wednesday, December 5

Dear Lee,

It's hard to answer the question, "How are you doing?" Or even harder, "How is retirement? Are you loving it?" I answer, "I'm managing" or "It's not what I expected." I want to say, "Are you seriously asking me this?" It's not people's fault. They don't understand. I can't expect them to. I have to let it go.

Love, Mom

Thursday, December 6

Dear Lee,

I feel so out of whack and aimless today. Is this holiday grief? It started just before Thanksgiving, the sadness wrapping around me like a wet, cold blanket I can't shed, trapping these feelings inside. I wish time to pass like never before.

My friend, Elaine, called tonight to tell me how you dropped in during a class she took. The medium said she usually doesn't allow a spirit to do this, but you were persistent, so she relented. You said, "Thank you for being my mom's friend." Just like that, blanket cast aside.

Love, Mom

Friday, December 7

Dear Lee,

This morning, in the shower, I heard, "It's time." I know what this means, but I don't want to do it. I don't want to go back and open those journals. I don't want to write this story. I start to cry and feel the fear rising. Then I hear, "Fifteen minutes. Set the timer." I say over and over, "Fifteen minutes. You can do it." I close my eyes and breathe to mentally prepare. I ask for help from my guides, angels, God, ancestors, you, and anyone else willing to help. And I do it. I read my words from January 2018. It feels like a lifetime ago, and yesterday at the same time.

Love, Mom

Saturday, December 8

Dear Lee,

I listened to the quiet this morning before I opened my eyes. I ask what you are doing with your day. I was surprised when I heard, "Tanzania riding with antelopes." Is Tanzania in Africa? Are there antelopes there? I check and find out, yes. I smile because you loved "Planet Earth." And so, begins our adventure game. I don't care if this is real or not, but I imagine you happy, wild, and free.

Love, Mom

Sunday, December 9

Dear Lee,

Your loss has stripped me to the core. I go within seeking understanding and truth and found God, right where he/she has always been, obscured by the layers of bullshit fed to me my entire life. But the truth was there the whole time. Now it's time for the seed to grow so it can be seen and shared. The truth, you now know.

Love, Mom

Monday, December 10

Dear Lee,

I have learned we are all connected, and any unkind words, actions, or even negative thoughts affect your energy, as well as the person you intend it for. I will be more careful with my thoughts and deeds.

Love, Mom

Tuesday, December 11

Dear Lee,

Amsterdam is where you are going today. I used to love to travel, but it doesn't interest me anymore. It's good to know I can go anywhere I want, once I cross.

Love, Mom

Wednesday, December 12

Dear Lee,

Sometimes when I feel somewhat okay, I feel guilty because I think I should be feeling sad. I try to avoid people because if they ask how I am doing, I don't know how to answer. Do I want them to think I'm okay, or do I want them to feel bad for me? It's confusing and difficult to navigate these feelings, so it's easier to just avoid people.

Love, Mom

Thursday, December 13

Dear Lee,

I feel like I'm a burn victim shedding my old skin and replacing it with a new one. It will never be a perfect and smooth skin, but a skin that will be real, beautiful, and authentic. And I will wear the scars, bumps, and imperfections proudly.

I started the book. I stopped after four pages because I was crying so hard. I feel weak and drained now. After lunch, I wrote a few more pages. It's mentally and physically exhausting. But I will keep going. Maybe it will help someone. Maybe it will help me. I'm reading David Allison's book, *Finding Davey*, which gave me the courage to start mine. David's book was channeled through his son, Davey. I hear, "See Mom, you've been doing this right along."

Love, Mom

Friday, December 14

Dear Lee,

Today we let go of your house. Dad and I went there this morning. It was emotional. I hear you say, "It's just a house. A thing." I know this, but I'm allowed to be sad. I go from room to room, but not the basement. I don't want to look there even though the coal furnace has been replaced. I can't go down there. I left a dime in the corner of the living room for good luck. I think about the day you bought it. You were so proud. Dad and I were proud of you, too. When I left, I put a little cross with your name on it by the steps. I send the couple thoughts of love, peace, and happiness, and I hear you say, "That's the spirit, Mom." And I think, "I wouldn't want anything else." I immediately hear, "I know, Mom." I then say, "Watch over them, Lee." You say you will, and the connection is over.

Love, Mom

Saturday, December 15

Dear Lee,

I asked my Facebook friends to do an act of kindness in your honor. I was pleased by the response. Even one small act of kindness sends a ripple out into the world. And it feels so good.

Love, Mom

Sunday, December 16

Dear Lee,

Why do people say, "Rest in Peace"? I may be wrong, but to me, it seems to imply that you are dead and buried in the ground resting until you are raised and judged. From what I have learned so far, no one is resting on the other side. The other side sounds busy, lively, and full of fun without the problems of this earthly life. I will try not to let it bother me.

Love, Mom

Monday, December 17

Dear Lee,

I wish I could ignore Christmas this year. There's no tree or decorations up. I think of last Christmas when you said that it was kind of silly that we exchanged gift certificates and we should do something to help others. I like this idea.

I meditated this morning and heard, "Ireland." That's one place Dad wants to go. I would go for him.

Alma (Lee's cousin) called me to tell me what happened to her in the car. That is pretty powerful stuff. Thank you for watching out for her. (Alma said she was texting while driving and felt a thump on the back of her head. She thought someone was hiding in the back seat, but it was empty. She went back to texting and felt a second thump even harder than the first one. She then thought of Lee and said, "Okay, Lee, I get it," and stopped texting.) Good work!

Love, Mom

Tuesday, December 18

Dear Lee,

In meditation, I imagined myself leading a local chapter of Helping Parents Heal. It felt right, but I will move slowly. I have nothing to lose and everything to gain. I felt tingles on my head, but please send a heart, so I know this is the right thing to do.

Love, Mom

Wednesday, December 19

Dear Lee,

I put a small tree on your grave. I wonder how Christmas is done in Heaven.

Love, Mom

Thursday, December 20

Dear Lee,

I read about a discovery today. It's a small dwarf planet nicknamed, Far Out. It is eleven billion miles from the sun, so it is far out. It's pinkish and takes about 1,000 years to make one trip around the sun. I feel sad, thinking about how we would be talking about this. Then the tingles start, and I feel you laughing and saying, "You have no idea." Someday we will see this together.

Love, Mom

Friday, December 21

Dear Lee,

I met Caroline Chang today. I found her through Helping Parents Heal. Her son, Kyle, passed from an illness. You passed unexpectedly. We weren't prepared. But then, can you ever be prepared to lose a child? It's just more shocking when you don't see it coming. You didn't see it coming either. You fell asleep and were escorted home by angels, where you were met by everyone who loves you. I miss you terribly, but I am glad you are happy and loved.

Love, Mom

Saturday, December 22

Dear Lee,

I felt joy, real joy today for the first time. I was in a department store elevator. I had a $100 gift card in my purse, but I wanted nothing. A woman stepped into the elevator. She told me she picked a card from the giving tree and she was going to buy a shirt for someone in need. I tell her about you and hand her the gift card. She called me an angel. I said I just want to honor you. She touched my cheek, hugged me, and said, "Bless you." The elevator door opened, and I walked away with so much joy and love in my heart. I know I was put in the path of this woman at just the right moment.

Love, Mom

Sunday, December 23

Dear Lee,

My cousin is in critical care with lung cancer. Soon, he will be joining the family in the next life. I wish him a happy, joyous family reunion. I don't know what he believes, and I wonder if he is scared. How much better it would be if he knew the truth.

Love, Mom

Monday, December 24

Dear Lee,

I try to think of today as just another day, but it's not working. We went to a family gathering tonight. I pretended I was okay. I'm glad to be home now, so I can stop pretending. I can't hear one more, "Merry Christmas." Will I ever be able to say it again?

I love and miss you so much tonight.

Love, Mom

Tuesday, December 25

Dear Lee,

It's the first Christmas without you. I lay in bed for a long time. I didn't want to get up, but I did for the grandkids. I had teddy bears made from your tee shirts for them. Luke made a cross ornament with your name on it for his parents. I hope the holidays will get easier.

Love, Mom

Wednesday, December 26

Dear Lee,

So glad Christmas is over, but then you don't need a holiday to be sad when your child has passed, do you?

My cousin is being taken off the ventilator, so it's only a matter of time before he crosses. I imagine the preparations are being made to welcome him home. I guess it's exciting from the spirit world's perspective. I wonder what it will be like when it's my time? I no longer fear death. I would welcome it but won't seek it, so don't worry.

Love, Mom

Thursday, December 27

Dear Lee,

As I woke, I saw clouds opening and a beautiful light shining through. I thought, "It's a new day." I felt like I was shedding some of the Christmas heaviness—a small breakthrough.

I caught some lights shimmering near the photo of my grandfather, or at least I thought I did. It was only for a second, so I can't be sure. I look around to try to figure it out. I walk up and down the hallway, hoping it would happen again. It didn't. I've never seen anything like this before. My mind says to doubt, but my heart wants to believe. I let my heart win.

Love, Mom

Friday, December 28

Dear Lee,

The respirator was taken out, and my cousin sat up. He joked with his family and kept staring, at a corner, near the ceiling, saying, "Awesome." I think his parents and five siblings must have parted the veil and given him a glimpse. Then he passed.

Love, Mom

Saturday, December 29

Dear Lee,

I feel so overwhelmed today. I needed to return something to the store and can't find the receipt, so I have a meltdown. I feel unglued, untethered. I keep losing things. I can't keep organized or focused. Is this "grief brain" ever going to end? I sit in the car and put on some music and meditate. I imagine a calm place with water, and I go there. I invite in the Holy Spirit for strength and guidance. It doesn't take long to feel better. Dad says he hopes I can get back to being me. I know he wants me to be okay. I tell him I will. But doesn't he realize the "old me" is gone? In time, he will see a new me, the real me, a better me, emerge.

Love, Mom

Sunday, December 30

Dear Lee,

Sometimes I feel so weak, alone, afraid, and shattered. Then other times, I feel like a fierce lion that will roar and make you proud. Grief is such a roller coaster of emotions, but I ride the ride. I have no choice. I'm belted in and can't get off.

Love, Mom

Monday, December 31

Dear Lee,

One year ago, today, was the last time I was with you. You came to the house, and we had appetizers and drinks. I look at where you sat and imagine you sitting there now. I try to think of our conversation that night, but my mind is blank.

Good riddance 2018.

Love, Mom

YEAR
TWO

January 2019

Tuesday, January 1

Dear Lee,

I'm glad to be out of 2018, but I still have to face your first anniversary.

I did make some intentions for the new year:

Finish the book.

Start the HPH group.

Meditate at least 15 minutes a day.

Write in my journal for at least 15 minutes a day.

Work out to feel better.

Get rid of stuff.

I will do what I can.

Happy New Year, Lee.

Love, Mom

Wednesday, January 2

Dear Lee,

I had a wonderful massage today. It's part of my healing plan. It gives me such a sense of peace. I hope it gives me the strength to face your anniversary.

Love, Mom

Thursday, January 3

Dear Lee,

There was an article in the paper about the hybrid bus project. You were excited about this new opportunity, and I am sorry you didn't get to see it through. I know you would have excelled. You had a great work ethic, which is why you kept getting awards at work. I'm sure you are shining in your new role across the veil. I try to imagine your life, your role, learning, growing, exploring, and expanding.

I called into Suzanne Giesemann's "Messages of Hope" radio show to ask about pre-cognitive dreams. I'm trying to figure out why I had that dream. Suzanne explained my soul was easing me into what was going to happen. She said our soul always knows because we are connected. She said it was a "gift" given to me to send me on my spiritual path, and the fact I am listening to shows about the afterlife confirms the gift. I can't call it a gift yet and maybe never will, but I can see it as an opportunity. Either way, I promise I won't let you down.

Love, Mom

Friday, January 4

Dear Lee,

I went to a funeral. The priest used the words "gone" and "resting." I watched people reciting the prayers having no idea what they were saying. I don't want to be part of this any longer.

Love, Mom

Saturday, January 5

Dear Lee,

I have felt you around a lot lately. So many tingles on my head. It feels like bugs crawling. Maybe you are with me as we near the first anniversary. Do you miss me as much as I miss you?

Love, Mom

Sunday, January 6

Dear Lee,

During meditation, I asked for a red rose. I'm not sure if I should be so specific, but I got my rose. I was reading, *What God Said,* by Neal Donald Walsh, and he talked about a rose blooming. I thought, "Is that my rose?" Why do I doubt?

Jay sees the number 34 all the time. Your youth football number. We were at his house watching football today, and just before halftime, number 34 made a 34-yard field goal with 34 seconds left. I will take it.

Love, Mom

Monday, January 7

Dear Lee,

This is the day your soul left this earth. On record, it's January 9, because that's the day we found you. But you came in on the seventh and left on the seventh. In some strange way, this brings some comfort.

I'm up at 6 a.m., trying to sort out my feelings. I am sad and my heart heavy, but I am not curled up in a nonfunctional ball like I thought I would be. In meditation, I ask for a butterfly sign, then think how silly. It is 16 degrees in New York, and the butterflies are long gone. Later, as I was waiting for my car to be serviced, I glanced at the television in time to see a butterfly. Then the screen is filled with butterflies. I believe you are staying close this week, sending us all the love, comfort, and support you can.

Thank you for the 34's tonight too. (I was reading and looked up just in time to see two football players, each wearing number 34 on the TV screen.)

All my love, Mom

Tuesday, January 8

Dear Lee,

On this day, last year, you were dead on your couch. I was having coffee at work and said how fortunate I was to have five beautiful, successful, and good kids (I still do). Why didn't I have a gut feeling something was wrong? I had the premonition in the shower and the dream, but I felt nothing was amiss when I needed to. Was I not meant to know? Were those things just meant to soften the blow? The pain of your loss is beyond anything imaginable.

I know you don't want me to suffer, and I am trying. You know I am. The sadness rolls in like a thick fog, but I will weather it. I know it will ease. But for now, I have to feel these feelings and let these tears flow. Let them wash away the pain and sorrow.

I forgot to cancel my dentist appointment, so I forced myself to go. I pictured you as a small boy, in this chair, with sunglasses on. You insisted on wearing them because you were so light-sensitive. I look out the window as a hawk lands on the tree. It sits there for the longest time. Did you send it? I got my answer, on the way home, when another hawk flew along the edge of the road, then crossed in front of my car. Is this your sign? I like it. I will be on the lookout for more.

Love, Mom

Wednesday, January 9

Dear Lee,

Today is the day my heart shattered in a million pieces. I was sure I wouldn't survive. I didn't want to survive. Time stopped. Nothing mattered. I cared for nothing or no one. Not even myself. Especially myself. Looking back now, I am thankful for the fog I existed in. It kept me going and protected me. Now a year has passed. I have survived. As I look back on this path of grief, I can see how far I've come. It hasn't been easy, but I am doing the work. I know you are proud of me. I've kept breathing, kept being, and I promise to continue. And I am proud of you in whatever you are doing on the other side.

I look at the photos of you, my parents, and dad's parents. I can feel the love surrounding me. I have love in my heart, too. Yes, there is pain and sadness. And yes, my tears have flowed today, but it's the price of love. I now know love like never before, and I send it out to all those who love and miss you today. I hope they discover the truth that you are not gone or resting in peace. You simply gave up your body and returned home. You are your true self now. I know you are healthy, happy, learning, loving, and "having the time of your life." I am grateful that you chose me to be your mom, and you were with me for thirty years.

I made the decision today to start a chapter of Helping Parents Heal. I feel you helped lead me to this group, and they helped me to survive, something I wasn't sure was possible. I will shift my focus and help other parents. I know it will help with my healing, too.

Goodnight, my beautiful son. I love you so much.

Love, Mom

Thursday, January 10

Dear Lee,

I reached out to the medium you dropped in on, to book a reading, and she had a cancellation for tonight. Maybe you orchestrated this. She said:

- You were with me at the cemetery when I put the Christmas tree there.
- She saw a couch and knew you were found there.
- You referred to the basement, and she saw a pipe.
- You showed her the blue and gold basketball sneakers.
- She asked about a BB gun, which you showed her lying in the grass. We found that empty box but no gun and had wondered where it was.

Thank you for tonight. It helps.

Love, Mom

Friday, January 11

Dear Lee,

The year of firsts is over. I don't expect things to be easier. Still, I won't be thinking, "It's the first Mother's Day, Father's Day, birthday, holiday, or whatever." I continue the work to heal this deep wound. And I will bear my scars and make you proud.

Love, Mom

Saturday, January 12

Dear Lee,

I wonder what you might have done if you knew you were going to transition? So, I decide to have you write a letter to me.

Dear Mom,

This is to let you know I will be leaving this realm of life. It's not my choice, but it's my time. Well, maybe not quite the time, but an opportunity came up, and I took it. Like I've said, I'm the happiest I've been in a long time. Summer and I struggled. I was a jerk. She endured my anger and depression as long as she could. I wasn't making her happy. How could I? I wasn't happy. You know some of my actions, but not all. It doesn't matter. But toward the end, I was becoming my old self, and I was happy. I came around more. Not as much as I wish I had, but I was beginning to. I know you wish you had come over for dinner, even if it was pizza. You waited to be invited. I'm sorry I never did. I'm sorry, too, that I ignored you when you did come by. I know you felt like my gaming was more important than you. It was, and it wasn't. I guess I was kind of selfish in the things I wanted to do. Being a grown-up was hard for me. I didn't like the responsibilities although I did what I had to do. My work ethic was good, so I got my shit done, then it was me time. I would do it differently now.

I want you to know how much I miss you and the family, but I am around even if no one feels me. I know you feel the tingles and wish it was more, but it's the best I can do right now.

I also want you to know how much I appreciate all you and Dad did for me. You watched over me, cared for me, and loved me. I know you still love me, and I love you more now than ever. And I can help and guide you from here, which I do. I am proud of you and the path you have taken. You are going to help people. Your words are already inspiring others.

I hope Dad can come to terms with my death. It was a stupid accident for sure, but a lot of good is coming from it and will continue to come like the poker tournament happening next month. Dad should go. And he should invite my buddies. I think they would like that.

My life here is amazing and wonderful. It's full of adventure and love. I know so many people, family, and friends. I love hearing family stories, going places, and hanging with friends.

Try not to be too sad because, as I tell you all the time, "I'm having the time of my life."

I love you, Mom

Lee

Sunday, January 13

Dear Lee,

I've been noticing more signs recently, and I think you are getting better at them. I sense you making your monkey face, and I hear, "I'm definitely good." Then I feel the tingles on my head. The voice in my head tries to say I'm making this up, but I'm not, so I tell the voice to be quiet. I know the truth. You are alive, and you are here. No one can tell me otherwise.

Love, Mom

Monday, January 14

Dear Lee,

I know gratitude is the remedy for grief. So here goes:

I am grateful you didn't suffer.

I am grateful I had you physically here for thirty years.

I am grateful you are well.

I am grateful you are happy.

I am grateful you are having the time of your life.

I am grateful for my six beautiful grandkids.

I am grateful for my wonderful kids.

I am grateful for my five siblings.

I am grateful I can get up each day.

I am grateful for my husband, and all he does for me.

I am grateful for the joy my bird brings me.

I am grateful I am well-off financially.

I am grateful we have plenty of food.

I am grateful for my friend, Deb, who stuck by me this entire time.

I am grateful Ruby is with you.

I am grateful for Sara, who guides and mentors me.

I am grateful I was led to Helping Parents Heal.

I am grateful for this spiritual path.

I am grateful for my guides and angels.

I am grateful for my family, friends, and ancestors.

I am grateful I had Ernie in my life for the first four months.

I am grateful to God.

I will practice gratitude every day from now on.

Love, Mom

Tuesday, January 15

Dear Lee,

I wake during the night thinking of you.

I hear, "I'm happier than I've ever been."

And I ask, "What do you do?"

You say, "Anything and everything."

I smile at the comfort this brings me.

Then you say, "Mom, be happy. Spread joy, love and help others."

Then I sleep well.

Love, Mom

Wednesday, January 16

Dear Lee,

I have heard that only part of our souls comes into human existence. Is this why we don't remember who we are and where we came from? Scientists say we only use a tiny bit of our brains, so it makes sense that we would only use part of our souls as well. I guess if the quantum physicists don't know, I sure won't figure it out. But I like the idea that part of me is with you and having the time of my life, too.

Love, Mom

Thursday, January 17

Dear Lee,

When I woke this morning and asked where you were going, I heard, "The White House" and "I can go anywhere." I know you found this funny.

Love, Mom

Friday, January 18

Dear Lee,

I tried to work on the book today, but it was too hard. I let the doubts creep in and had to stop. I know you wanted it for your first anniversary, but I just couldn't do it.

Love, Mom

Sunday, January 20

Dear Lee,

I've avoided going back to the day but, maybe I should. Maybe I have to go through it and feel it fully, so I can let it go.

Love, Mom

Monday, January 21

Dear Lee,

Today's adventure is the Vatican. Oh, the places you are going.

Love, Mom

Tuesday, January 22

Dear Lee,

This morning when I asked what you were doing, I sensed Buddy and Ruby with you as I heard, "Mt. Everest." I love this game.

I listened to a speaker tonight on a Helping Parents Heal meeting. He said becoming soul-centered helps you to heal. He said to embrace who your child is now rather than focusing on who he or she was in the physical. This makes sense to me. I feel this may be the nudge I needed to continue on this path. Please help me to understand this so I can move forward. I trust your love and guidance. Thank you for validating this with the tingles.

Love, Mom

Wednesday, January 23

Dear Lee,

Early on in my grief, I mourned the death of me, as well as you, knowing I would never be the same. Now I sit here, one year later, celebrating my new self, the one who has been awakened, made new, and is aware of the oneness of life.

Love, Mom

Thursday, January 24

Dear Lee,

Why does it take a tragedy to awaken?

Love, Mom

Friday, January 25

Dear Lee,

In meditation this morning, I sent out love to all the parents that are just starting this grief journey. I hope they can hold on.

Love, Mom

Saturday, January 26

Dear Lee,

When I think of you as a free spirit, living without pain or trials of any kind, I am kind of jealous. My mind can't fathom the bliss and joy of the next life if it's anything like I've read. And I hear, "Oh, it is." And I feel the tingles.

Love, Mom

Sunday, January 27

Dear Lee,

I imagined a garden in meditation this morning. I met you, Ruby, Buddy, my parents, Dad's parents, and my grandparents. I felt such joy, peace, and love in my heart. I felt a connection to the hundreds or thousands of people, known and unknown, who are connected to me. Meditation is remarkable.

Love, Mom

Monday, January 28

Dear Lee,

Antarctica was the first thing I heard when I woke up. I think about you exploring there or going anywhere you want.

Love, Mom

Tuesday, January 29

Dear Lee,

Sometimes I feel the pull of the questions like why or how. I try not to, but they lurk, at the edges, of my human mind. I work hard to overrule these thoughts because they are pointless and don't change reality. Thank you for proving you are right here with the tingles. They help. I am starting to accept you as you exist now.

Love, Mom

Wednesday, January 30

Dear Lee,

I watched you in the fall of 2017, but it wasn't out of fear. It was something different that I couldn't name. You seemed different to me somehow. Maybe our souls knew something our human minds could not have known.

Love, Mom

Thursday, January 31

Dear Lee,

I woke up at 4:30 a.m. and thought, "There's a reason" and heard, "There's always a reason, Mom."

Love, Mom

February 2019

Friday, February 1

Dear Lee,

Many good things will happen in your honor. The first thing is we are setting up a scholarship at your high school. I was thinking of someone going to Clarkson, like you, but I'm not sure. It will be for someone who, like you, has a strong work ethic. I know you will direct me.

Love, Mom

Sunday, February 3

Dear Lee,

It's Super Bowl Sunday, and I'm having a low day. I don't care about football anymore, and maybe in your new life, you don't either. But what I am missing is the silly, goofy banter between you and Jay. It's something only siblings do. I will let the sadness ooze out of me today.

Love, Mom

Monday, February 4

Dear Lee,

Interesting conversation in the car today with Haydan (three-year-old).

It went like this:

Haydan: "Oma, are you talking to yourself?"

Me: "No, I'm talking to Uncle Lee."

Haydan: "Uncle Lee is dead."

Me: "He's not dead. He's only left his body. He is alive, so I can still talk to him. We just can't see him."

Haydan: "Can I talk to Uncle Lee?"

I said she could and handed her your picture. She holds it and sings the Beatles', "Blackbird." Then she describes what she sees out the window.

Can I help change people's views of death? I will try one conversation at a time.

Love, Mom

Wednesday, February 6

Dear Lee,

I think about how many people were affected by your "death." How many are sad. You tell me your soul knew to take the exit and not to be sad. To trust. Believe. Accept. It's hard to trust because it's hard to accept, but I try. (tingles)

Love, Mom

Thursday, February 7

Dear Lee,

The money from the poker tournament tonight will be used to buy detectors. Dad had a picture of you both, seated at the same table, from a few years ago. Then after the draw for tonight's seating, the same people ended up at Dad's table, with one chair empty. How does that happen? Coincidence? I hardly think so.

Love, Mom

Saturday, February 9

Dear Lee,

I know you've only gone home a little before me, so all I have to do is hold on. And I will. I have to. I will do this for you. I will do this for me. I will do this for my family. And I will do this for other parents who will come after me. They will need a place, a group, a tribe of wounded people who will hold on together.

Love, Mom

Sunday, February 10

Dear Lee,

I'm excited about becoming an Affiliate Leader for Helping Parents Heal. I believe I can help others, and by doing so, I will help myself. I even feel some joy, which I didn't want to admit to myself, but I need to feel every feeling that arises. A cardinal flew in front of my car a short while ago, as if to confirm you are aware and pleased.

Love, Mom

Monday, February 11

Dear Lee,

I heard "Nebula" this morning, so I looked it up. It's a cloud of gas in space. The images are beautiful. I can only imagine what it looks like from your perspective. I'll know someday.

Love, Mom

Tuesday, February 12

Dear Lee,

"Sahara" is what I heard as I woke. I imagine you and your friends riding on camels across the desert. What a time you must be having.

Love, Mom

Wednesday, February 13

Dear Lee,

I read that, from a spiritual perspective, human life is short. A soul can be playing poker, then come into a human body and be back in time for the next hand. That's hard to wrap my mind around since time here seems to drag.

Love, Mom

Thursday, February 14

Dear Lee,

I didn't expect Valentine's Day to affect me. You would say that it's a stupid Hallmark Day. But I am sad because I am missing the physical you, the one I can hug. So, I will go within and imagine you sending me love straight to my heart. And I will let my tears fall as they need to. I will expel them and let them flow because they are healing me from the inside out. And I will teach others not to hold them back because they are necessary for healing.

I love you!

Love, Mom

Friday, February 15

Dear Lee,

In meditation this morning, you told me how proud you are of me. How well I am doing. You see me trying my best. I do have moments of joy. I have survived the worst thing a parent could ever endure. I'm proud of myself, too.

Love, Mom

Saturday, February 16

Dear Lee,

I think of your child, in spirit. I can feel how proud you are of him. You are teaching him things. Maybe you take him to my cousin, the professor, in the Halls of Learning. The lessons might be a little over his head, but I'm sure he doesn't mind because he is with you. Tell him I love him.

Love, Mom

Sunday, February 17

Dear Lee,

The most interesting thing happened today. The family was here. Dad had the Daytona 500 on to watch his favorite driver, Michael McDonald. Car 34 was in the lead with 34 seconds to go. And Michael is 34 years old. We all looked at each other in disbelief. I had goosebumps. And as I write this, I have tingles on my head. Thank you for reminding me you were with us, and all is in perfect order.

Love, Mom

Tuesday, February 19

Dear Lee,

Surrender popped into my head this morning. I know the only way to find the healing and peace I seek is to surrender to God. I will quiet the chatter in my mind, go within to the quiet place, where I find my truth and strength, which comes from the love existing there. And I will surrender. You have given me this opportunity, and for this, I am grateful.

Love, Mom

Wednesday, February 20

Dear Lee,

I'm on my way to see Uncle Don before I head to the We Don't Die conference in Boston, hosted by Sandra Champlain. I've never been to anything like this, so I have no idea what to expect. I'm anxious to see Don, who has been through a lot, with his lung cancer.

As I drive along, I ask you for signs you are traveling with me. And when I glance at my odometer, it ends in 34, then the next mile marker I see is mile 34. Thank you for being my companion.

Love, Mom

Friday, February 22

Dear Lee,

As I drove to Boston today, I kept thinking I made a mistake. I wanted to be home. I was excited to go, but I'm not so sure now. Maybe I'm not ready.

Love, Mom

Saturday, February 23

Dear Lee,

I'm so glad I came to the conference. The energy is great. It's a mixed bag of people, so not everyone is a parent who has had a child pass. I've met so many terrific people, and the speakers are awesome. I'm learning a lot. It's incredible to be with people who believe in the afterlife and communication with spirit. I feel at home with them. Thank you for the tingles.

My roommate, Caroline, tells me to take some pictures to catch an orb tonight. I'm not sure I believe in orbs, but I take some pictures. Suddenly, a light shot from the lower-left corner to the top right corner of the room. I'm not sure what to make of it, but I know what I saw.

Love, Mom

Sunday, February 24

Dear Lee,

Today was mind-blowing. I did a meditation with Kerry McLeod and Philip Dykes. I saw a kaleidoscope of purple and green, as I often do, but then I saw an orange image pushing through the purple. It was you. I recognized your features. My impulse was to open my eyes, but I knew if I did, you'd be gone. So, I hung on with tears falling down my face. But this was only the beginning. I signed up for a reading with Jane Seybold right after the meditation. You stepped right in and told Jane I was "bitching" about coming to the conference. I told her I wasn't "bitching," but

I did have second thoughts. She said, "No. He says you were bitching. I relented.

- You said my life was a new beginning, and I was going to help people with a group that would be bigger than I imagined.
- You said, "Zoom, zoom." Does that mean to get right on it or something else?
- We both had a *"knewing,"* and you were aware I was watching you.
- Jane saw a horse. I wasn't sure at first, but then I remembered Anne, who is making the quilts, has horses.

After the reading, I felt like I had been fried or electrocuted. I went back to the conference, but everything around me felt surreal. I can't explain it, but I didn't feel like I was here anymore. I decided to go back to my room. I sobbed for the longest time, and these words came:

Dear Mom,

Don't be afraid. You will help people because of the depth of your experience with grief. My gift, your gift, it's the same gift, a messy, beautiful gift, a necessary gift. You need to let it out. The sobbing is healing you. But your eyes, heart, and soul are now opened to the truth. There's no turning back. Have no fear. Go forward. Be fearless. Love deeply. Now there's work to be done—great fun to channel on the toilet. Trust me. Don't get caught up in doubt.

I love you, Mom.

Lee

Jane had told me I had come to find answers, and I had found them. She said you had come to me, in meditation, to help me see that you are alive in spirit, and to give me the knowledge and strength to see my path. I know now spirit set this all up. It validates everything. I was spent, then I heard, "You're done. Mission accomplished." I packed up early and went home.

Love, Mom

Monday, February 25

Dear Lee,

In meditation this morning, I realized I was given a gift. I can't believe I am even thinking this, but I have somehow shifted from 'opportunity' to 'gift.' Is this feeling temporary? What will people think if I say your death was a gift? And with these thoughts, I have a vision of a door with a big padlock, which is broken. The door is open slightly, and there is brilliant light spilling through. And while the door isn't fully open, there is enough room to walk through, and I do.

I feel like I have turned a corner or shed some old skin. I'm not saying I am healed, but I do see the path. Do I wish with all my heart that you were here? Would I give anything to have that? Absolutely. But I know you are by my side. You have made the ultimate sacrifice for my soul to progress, so I will not waste it. I will do my best to find my purpose and use my gifts to help others.

Love, Mom

Tuesday, February 26

Dear Lee,

What I found at the We Don't Die conference was the courage to go forward. My grief has shifted and lifted slightly. I will continue to do the work. I will always miss you, Lee, but I am now full of courage, strength, love and truth. I wear these now as a banner. I feel your tingles. I hear your thoughts. This is real. This is forever.

Love, Mom

Wednesday, February 27

Dear Lee,

Thinking about the book today, I thought, "I'm afraid it won't be enough." And I heard, "You're not writing the great American novel, you know. It's just our story. Lose the fear." 'Okay, teacher.'

Love, Mom

Thursday, February 28

Dear Lee,

My heart is full of so much gratitude today.

I am grateful for my warm house.

I am grateful for the weekend I spent learning about the afterlife.

I am grateful for the meditation where I saw you.

I am grateful for the reading with Jane.

I am grateful for the tingles letting me know you hear me.

I am grateful for your communication in my head.

I am grateful for Sara, who has guided me.

I am grateful for Helping Parents Heal, which has saved me.

I am grateful for having you in my life for 30 years.

I am grateful you chose me to be your mom.

I am grateful for the signs you send.

I am grateful you are happy.

I am grateful you are free to explore without restriction.

I am grateful you are my cheerleader.

I am grateful to have survived the worst thing ever to happen to me.

I am grateful to know the love I have found at my core.

I am simply grateful.

Love, Mom

March 2019

Friday, March 1

Dear Lee,

I still struggle with the idea of a soul plan even though I know life continues. I question my purpose now. What purpose did your death serve? I know I have come away with more compassion and love, so maybe that is all it is. Maybe I don't have to do something spectacular. Maybe I just have to simply help others.

Love, Mom

Saturday, March 2

Dear Lee,

During meditation, I imagined a bench in a beautiful garden. You were sitting there with Buddy and Ruby. I sat down next to you and Ruby put her head in my lap. My dad stepped in and said my name. Then lots of relatives came into my vision. So many surrounded us with love. I saw Jesus' mother, Mary, who took my hands and said she knows my heart, but the shattered pieces are mending, and I will bear my scars well. I am so comforted by this.

Love, Mom

Sunday, March 3

Dear Lee,

An unexpected thing happened during today's meditation; I saw two local young people who were murdered. I didn't know them, even though the young man graduated with you. It came as a surprise when he said, "It's like a friggin' S.V. (Susquehanna Valley High School) reunion sometimes." I've never had anything like this happen before, but I decide to share it with his mom. She says it's exactly how he would say it. I don't know how this all works, but I will be open to it.

Love, Mom

Monday, March 4

Dear Lee,

The snow is falling lightly. It looks like a postcard. And I think how a postcard is not real, like this life. (tingles) I find it comforting to think of the afterlife as real life, and this life is for learning our lessons, loving and growing. Why doesn't humanity know this? "That's the lesson," I hear you say. We have to figure this out, one by one. I understand that my wake-up call and knowing, is the gift, but why does the lesson have to hurt this much? I wish it could have come another way. And I hear, "It's the way it was meant to be." Then I hear, "Zoom, zoom." What am I supposed to do?

Love, Mom

Tuesday, March 5

Dear Lee,

I woke at 3:43 a.m., with these whispered words, "Get on the book. Trust. Believe. No worries. Just go for it." I wanted to go back to sleep, but I get up and meditate. I am back on the bench. Our feet are in the water. Everything is warm and beautiful.

"Isn't this the best place ever? You can do so much. Anything you want."

All I can think is, "Hold on, hold on, hold on."

I wrote another letter from you today:

Dear Mom,

You think something is missing in your life because I'm not there physically, but you are wrong. I am with you and want the connection to be stronger and more consistent, but you still have a shimmer of doubt around you. I say doubt because if you truly believed, then you would be joyful in knowing all is well and as it should be. But this is hard for a parent to do. I see the sadness in you. I know you are trying as hard as you can, and you have done well. But it's like two steps forward and one back. Keep trying. There will be progress.

I know it hurts when you are asked how you are enjoying retirement like you could have forgotten about me or "moved on" and having the time of your life. It's okay to say you are glad to have the time to process your grief to try to heal. That is all you need to say.

You know that I am with you. Trust me to guide you. My love for you is stronger than ever.

Love always,

Lee

Wednesday, March 6

Dear Lee,

I wasn't sleeping so got up to meditate, and these words came:

I'm so happy and busy. I can go anywhere, visit anyone, see planets, galaxies, whatever. Fill the hole in your heart with love. Love will ease the pain. When pain creeps in, seek love by helping others. It's the best way to survive the grief. Don't let grief take you down. Grief destroys if not felt. Love rises like a balloon taking you to places you can't imagine, unless you're here, of course. (I'm sure you are laughing at this.)

This was not planned in the way you think, but a lot of good has and will come of my death, so focus on that.

When you deflate with pain, inflate with love.

Love,

Lee

As morning lights up, I look at the sky. It is so blue. The sun is out. I am grateful for the cold, which you no longer feel. And my day begins.

Love, Mom

Thursday, March 7

Dear Lee,

It's still hard to run into people I know. I know they are unsure of what to say. Do they mention "it?" They are afraid to. Once upon a time, I was too. They don't say your name, and it hurts.

I want to tell them:

"Don't be afraid to say my loved one's name, thinking that you will hurt me.

For though the pain has lodged in my heart, these tears are healing ones, formed to ebb away my jagged edges, smoothing them into a thing of beauty."

Love, Mom

Friday, March 8

Dear Lee,

I'm trying to learn to be more present without looking behind or ahead. Meditation is a place where I have learned this and a place where I find the most comfort. Thank you for being there with me, Lee.

Love, Mom

Saturday, March 9

Dear Lee,

It's interesting when I wake up, in the middle of the night, with a complete thought in my head. I write it down, so I don't forget, then read it in the morning. Is this a download?

This is what I wrote:

"Today, I will rise and be a new self, a better self, a gentler self. This new self, carved out of pain and suffering, now turns to others to wipe away their tears."

Love, Mom

Sunday, March 10

Dear Lee,

When I look at your picture, I now see the old soul in your eyes. I knew you were different from the rest, but I didn't understand this from a spiritual perspective. To know this, at the human level, would have been unbearable. I wasn't ready. Now I'm ready.

Love, Mom

Tuesday, March 12

Dear Lee,

Another download from you:

"Bravo, bravo, and bravo again. Do you know how proud I am of you? You are doing so well and will do great things. I love you so much, and I am with you every step of the way. Take the steps. Be fearless. We've got this together. Take my hand and let me lead you on your path."

I thank you for these words. I will not doubt or be bothered by the doubters. I know some will think I'm crazy, but I don't care. Some might be scared for my soul, sure that some evil or devil has gotten hold of me. All kinds of things might be thought of me, but I no longer care. They can walk away from me, pray for me, feel sorry for me, or whatever, but I know the truth. And I will speak it.

Love, Mom

Wednesday, March 13

Dear Lee,

When I woke, I looked at your picture and said, good morning, as I do every day. I felt the tingles on my head, and I know it's you.

"I know you are here, Lee." "Thank you. I love you."

"I love you too, Mom."

"Thank you for coming to me, but I don't like it that you aren't here. I know you hug me."

"Yeah, I wasn't a big hugger before, and I'm sorry."

"It's okay, honey," I say.

"Mom, it's such bullshit there. So much better here. You'll see."

"It's hard to wait. It could be a long time."

"It's not. You'll be fine."

"I love you, Lee. Thank you."

And I get up to write.

Love, Mom

Thursday, March 14

Dear Lee,

It's the first warm day, and I am sitting outside. I feel the warmth of the sun. I watch the birds. I notice the buds on the trees. And I think, "Did I notice any of this last year?" I think about the many manhunt games played in this yard. I'm grateful for this peek into the past. It brings me comfort like this sweatshirt of yours I'm wearing. I'm grateful I can feel these things again.

Love, Mom

Friday, March 15

Dear Lee,

I was at the store today. Someone I knew turned away, pretending they didn't see me. It happens a lot. I want to say to them that I understand. It's okay. Sometimes I like to be a ghost.

Love, Mom

Saturday, March 16

Dear Lee,

One minute I am doing fine, but in a blink of an eye, it crumbles. Sometimes I don't even know the trigger. I've been handed the proof that life continues from readings, books, and podcasts. I was blown away, by the proof, at the conference. How do you keep the knowing going? How do you keep the doubt from creeping back in?

Two steps forward, one step back.

Inflate. Deflate. Inflate. Repeat.

Love, Mom

Sunday, March 17

Dear Lee,

Happy St. Patrick's Day. It's 10 a.m., and I'm alone at the cemetery with a Guinness, in my hand. I have a toast and drink half, then pour the rest on your grave. I ask for a sign and see a 34 on a mailbox. Thank you.

The family is coming over for boiled dinner. You loved the boiled dinner. What do you like better, boiled dinner or clam chowder?

Everyone is here. I silently ask you to send a sign to us, like blinking the lights or messing with the TV. Then suddenly, the glass with the burning candle breaks. I'm not sure this is the sign, but I will believe just in case.

Love, Mom

Monday, March 18

Dear Lee,

I understand my healing will be a life-long commitment. This must be why you never get "over it," but you learn how to manage your grief. I'm willing to do the work. To the world, I may look like I'm doing okay, but on the inside, I'm doing some hard work.

Love, Mom

Tuesday, March 19

Dear Lee,

I imagined the tears that fell, in meditation, bathing my heart with healing. My mind started to spin away with all the things I wanted to do today. I hear, "Slow down. Be present and let things unfold rather than trying to manipulate them." I'm not sure if these words come from you or my guides, but it doesn't matter. I realize I'm trying to make things happen rather than letting them unfold. I need to trust the process.

Love, Mom

Wednesday, March 20

Dear Lee,

I had a wonderful massage today. I asked for Sheehan's hands to be blessed by her guides and helpers. I meditated and prayed and felt the energy of healing around me. I will continue this self-care because I know it's important for healing.

Love, Mom

Thursday, March 21

Dear Lee,

The most incredible thing happened last night. I went to bed at 9:54 p.m. and fell right asleep. I was startled awake when it felt like someone getting into the bed behind me. I thought, "Why is Tom getting into bed on my side?" Then something started bouncing all around the bed. I felt Dad's side, but he wasn't there. I was a little frightened at first, thinking something was on the bed, so I laid still. I thought, Aya? (My cockatiel.) But no, Aya is in his cage. A mouse? This was too heavy for a mouse. Suddenly, I thought, "Ruby?" (Our family dog who passed in 2011.) Then I knew this was a real visit. It had happened before, but I dismissed it as my imagination. Not this time. Thank you for the beautiful visit, Ruby. Thank you for sending her, Lee.

I love you both!

Mom

Friday, March 22

Dear Lee,

I decided I like the term "hereafter" over "afterlife." Afterlife is somewhere you go after "real" life, which I now know you didn't go anywhere. Hereafter means you are right here just existing in a different form, which is comforting. I know you aren't gone. I know you are here.

Love, Mom

Saturday, March 23

Dear Lee,

Another young person I know has passed. I didn't want to go to the funeral parlor, but I did. I was okay until someone says, "This must be so hard for you." I start to cry, and I hear, "You've got this, Mom." Thank you for letting me know you are with me.

Love, Mom

Monday, March 25

Dear Lee,

I wake up at 3:30 a.m. with these words. I write them down in the dark.

I am here to fill your heart with love.

Can you feel me?

Do you know me?

Don't be afraid.

Don't be sad.

Carry my love with you.

Give it to others.

In morning meditation, I ask God, my angels, guides, ancestors, family, and you to bathe me with love, compassion, strength, and guidance. I feel my sadness diminish and a power brewing in me, like a storm on the horizon. I will make you proud. I can do this.

Love, Mom

Tuesday, March 26

Dear Lee,

In a Helping Parents Heal meeting tonight, the medium was asked why so many young people are dying from substance abuse. She said that sometimes a large group of kids volunteer to leave, to demonstrate the need for change. She said humans have lost our way and need to be reminded. Things like substance abuse deaths and tragedies like we've seen in schools and other public places are reminders that we are not following our spiritual path. We are caught up in our human story, forgetting who we truly are. This seems drastic, but it makes sense, too. I prefer thinking this rather than thinking what we call "bad things" are senseless and random.

Love, Mom

Wednesday, March 27

Dear Lee,

It's been an emotional day. I just went with it. I can get in and get out easier now. I can breathe my way through the pain. I can replace the image of when we found you, with a good memory. I focus on the picture of you on your 30th birthday. I can do this. I can bear the pain of missing you physically because I know we don't die. I am fortunate to know this.

Love, Mom

Friday, March 29

Dear Lee,

"Good morning, Lee," I say as I open my eyes and look at the drawing of us. "Where today?" is my next thought. And immediately, I hear, "Bermuda." I love this game of connection. Thank you for playing with me.

Today I picked out the material for the back of the quilts. Ann and I walked into the house converted into a store. It was packed with material, but I had a feeling to turn left. I was looking for something blue, as you directed. I spotted it right away: a dark blue, star-filled material. "This is it," I said to Ann. "Are you sure you don't want to look around?" she asked. "Nope." I knew you led me to the perfect material. When the quilt is finished, I will sleep under the stars every night.

Love, Mom

Saturday, March 30

Dear Lee,

I had coffee with a mom whose son passed, and she mentions a mutual friend I haven't seen in quite some time, then I ran into her tonight. No coincidences, right?

Love, Mom

Sunday, March 31

Dear Lee,

Thank you for the signs today. I wasn't sure about the heart-shaped pothole in the road, so I turned around to make sure I saw it. Then a 34 on a mailbox. Then I turn on *60 Minutes*, and there's a story about grieving parents. But Dad's crossword was the best. He got lees (ashes in a woodstove) and Chuck Norris. As they say, you can't make this up. Thank you and I love you.

Love, Mom

April 2019

Monday, April 1

Dear Lee,

I haven't read a fiction book since you passed, but I've read about 50 books on spirituality, afterlife, and grief. I don't know if I will ever read fiction again.

Love, Mom

Tuesday, April 2

Dear Lee,

I got a beautiful trance healing message from Ann:

"Slow down, love. The swirling energy around you tempts you to partake, but instead step aside and allow it to float by. This is not your tidal wave to get caught up in. Release it to us, and we, in turn, will provide the cushion with which to sit and regroup. This timing is all about you. The number 2 comes in around an anniversary or other upcoming events. Again, surrender any stress to us. We are here to take it away. Make no mistake; we have another agenda to align you on the path that you were meant for. Don't slip away, embrace it, and walk with us. You won't be disappointed. With love."

I think about this message, and I wonder if I am moving too fast with a Helping Parents Heal chapter. I need to trust that the spirit world will present the right time to me. And I write:

Dear spirit world,

I am ready to know me. Show me what you know about me. I don't remember. I ask for your support and guidance.

Thank you for serving me.

Love, Mom

Wednesday, April 3

Dear Lee,

I've been invited to a Mother's Day Retreat at Omega Institute in Rhinebeck, N.Y. It's a special retreat for moms whose kids have passed. It was organized by a mom who works there. Cynthia Campbell's daughter, Desiree, passed soon after you. It's called Desiree's Gathering. Speakers and mediums have volunteered their time and talents for us. I am grateful to be a part of this special weekend.

Love, Mom

Thursday, April 4

Dear Lee,

Another early morning download:

"Don't focus on the details of my death. It doesn't matter. It just is. Focus instead on the present and what is. You will experience joy again. Fan the flame. Let it burn bright."

Love, Mom

Friday, April 5

Dear Lee,

I spent time with my friend, Yvonne, today. She is spiritual, an R.N., and a grief counselor. I told her, in the beginning, I wanted to die. Her friend said she was "un-suicidal" in the beginning. You wish you were dead but would take no action. This describes it perfectly.

Love, Mom

Saturday, April 6

Dear Lee,

I'm outside watching three hawks fly around. They are so majestic. I love to watch them glide. I wished for them to fly closer to me, and two of them did. I'd like to think you directed them to me.

Love, Mom

Sunday, April 7

Dear Lee,

My brother mentioned it was painful to see me so broken when you passed. I think about my brokenness and how hard I've worked to put the pieces back together. I hope our book will help another parent who is broken. I hope that my words will help them see they can put their broken pieces back together if they want to. The pieces won't fit perfectly, but they will hold because the glue is love. Grief is full-time work. In the beginning, the dark despair was exhausting and all-consuming. Relief only came in small snippets, mostly in naps. But doing the work may save your life.

Love, Mom

Monday, April 8

Dear Lee,

Caitlin says she has a reoccurring dream. You and some friends are sitting at a bar having a good time. You are drinking a Fosters. She asks what you are doing, and you tell her, "Just hanging out." She tells you, "Your mom has been trying to get hold of you." You reply, "Oh, shit. Really?" You pat your pockets, feeling for your cellphone, which, of course, you don't have. You say, "Oh shit. I don't have my phone. Oh well, just let her know I'm doing just fine." Caitlin tells me she saw your smile and heard your laugh. "He's okay," she tells me. She said, "It's like he's out at the bar chillin' and havin' a good time and isn't ready to go home to talk yet."

This sure sounds like you.

Love, Mom

Wednesday, April 10

Dear Lee,

I woke up at 3:30 a.m. with the song, "In Heaven, there is no beer. That's why we drink it here." I hear rowdy laughter. "If only they knew," someone says. More laughter. "Save me a seat," I think.

Love, Mom

Thursday, April 11

Dear Lee,

Today is April's birthday. Send your sister a sign today. She needs it.

Love, Mom

Saturday, April 13

Dear Lee,

I wrote these words in the dark during the night.

"Without warning, the sadness rolls in like a thick fog. It covers me, making it hard to see or move forward. Nothing to do, but wait for it to pass and trust that the sun will break through it when it's time."

Love, Mom

Sunday, April 14

Dear Lee,

When I saw your image among the "unknowns" in Sonia Rinaldi's experiment, it took my breath away. (Sonia is a Brazilian researcher who brings through the voices and images of loved ones.) I briefly met Sonia in Boston, but I didn't tell her about you. I was skeptical about her work. It seemed "out there," too sci-fi, but I decided to be open. I guess you showed me. The image of you was about age ten or twelve. I'm not sure why you appeared, at that age, but I know it's you. I posted a picture of you on her Facebook page, where Lisa Laniewski, who works for Sonia, saw it and brought it to her attention. Sonia confirmed it's you, then asked about the dog in the image. I hadn't noticed one, so I looked, and there was Buddy, above your right shoulder. I don't know how this all works, but I don't have to. I believe. I went to We Don't Die Boston and Lisa went to the one in Orlando, but through your image, Lisa and I have connected. And we discovered you and Lisa's daughter, Amber, also in spirit, share a birthday.

Thank you, Lee and Amber.

Love, Mom

Monday, April 15

Dear Lee,

I turned on the radio and Offspring's "Why Don't You Get a Job" is playing. Then a Red Hot Chili Peppers song came on. I switch the station, and there is another Chili Peppers song. The song ends, and a song called "Happier," came on. I don't know this song, but when I hear the line, "I want you to be happier," I know it's a message from you. When I tell April about this, she says, "Hailey is singing this song for chorus." Once again, no coincidences.

Love, Mom

Tuesday, April 16

Dear Lee,

Even with the proof, the believing and the knowing that life continues, it's just so hard sometimes. I can't think about all the years I might live without you. I try to stay present. I try to be grateful that you were here physically here for thirty years. But the sadness sometimes washes it all away. I ask my angels to hold me up for the rest of my life because I'm not sure I can do this. Un-suicidal. Yep, that's me.

Love, Mom

Thursday, April 18

Dear Lee,

I did a past life regression and saw three lives, at different times. Like the EVP's, I'm not sure how I feel about this. It was interesting, though. I guess if we live forever and come here to learn lessons, then I guess multiple lives would make sense. I wish you could tell me.

Love, Mom

Tuesday, April 23

Dear Lee,

Our lawyer's son has passed. I wish I could take away his parents' pain, but all I can do is send them love and light.

Love, Mom

Wednesday, April 24

Dear Lee,

In meditation, I dipped my toes in a pool, when I should be plunging in. I know this relates to writing the book. Why do I hold back? What is my fear? That no one will believe me? Why does it matter? It's my story, my truth. What matters is my intention to help. I will ask for guidance. I know you and my guides are waiting to help. All I need to do is ask.

Love, Mom

Thursday, April 25

Dear Lee,

I found the receipt from the addiction center. It was from 2011, the year after you graduated from college. I know you used it in college, but I didn't realize you continued to take it, at least at first. I think by the time you realized that you had a problem, you were in too deep. I'm sorry you didn't feel you could come to me. I regret I didn't challenge you, but I was afraid of pushing you away. You were already hard to reach, so if you acted fine, I pretended all was well, even though my heart told me differently. But in the end, you overcame that demon. What you did was remarkable. I am so proud of you.

Love, Mom

Friday, April 26

Dear Lee,

A bird hit the sliding glass door today. I've been talking to you all day, so I hope you sent it. I will take it as a sign since it flew off and was okay.

Love, Mom

Sunday, April 28

Dear Lee,

When you have a baby, you know love like you've never known it before. You can't explain it to anyone, but it's real. But you don't understand how deep and profound the love is until your child passes. What happens when a parent doesn't understand their relationship can continue, and they can connect with their child? Do they suffer more as a result? I wasn't willing to let you go. I had to connect somehow. The pain and love now connect us more than ever before.

Love, Mom

Monday, April 29

Dear Lee,

This has been a day of signs. I turn on the radio, in the car, and "Happier" is playing. I look at the clock, and it's 6:34 a.m. Then I see two more 34's, one on a mailbox and my car says it's 34 degrees outside. Then I see two more 34's, on mailboxes. I am grateful for these signs.

Love, Mom

May 2019

May 1

Dear Lee,

I dropped off a book and card for our lawyer. I started feeling overwhelmed and weepy. I let the tears come because it's the only way. Then I stop for gas, and the pump stops at $34. This is how it works.

Love, Mom

May 2

Dear Lee,

I heard from you first thing upon waking:

"Today's the day. I have something to tell you."

I ask, "Can you tell me now?"

"No, Isabella will share."

(I had a reading scheduled with Isabella Johnson at 6:30 p.m. It was hard to wait.)

6:30 p.m.

Isabella was giving her introduction when Lee burst in. She asked, "Do you have a son in spirit?"

I said, "Yes, I do."

"Well, he's here, and he's chomping at the bit."

I wasn't surprised. I could feel the excitement building all afternoon.

Isabella's validations were on point, and some highlights are:

- He just fell asleep and woke up on the other side.
- He is weird and goofy, but smart.
- He mentioned a big event coming up (a family wedding this weekend) and shows himself in a tux but says, "It's not that formal. I look good, though."
- He showed Isabella a detector and says, "Thank you for handing them out."
- He mentions he likes my new haircut.
- My mom has the soul baby. She loves listening to him talk, but it goes over her head.
- He says he wishes he had more balance in his life, but self-acceptance was his lesson to learn.
- Isabella asked if I've been noticing different birds lately. I tell her that I've been seeing a lot of hawks. She holds up a paper where she had written the word "hawk."
- He mentions a good buddy (JT) and says he is like a brother. "Tell him I'm okay. Tell him I love him." He said he wouldn't have said that in life, but can now.
- He talked about Summer and said he appreciates and has gratitude for the experience of the relationship. She broke his heart. He loved her, but she wanted to play "house," and he was focused on other things.
- He showed her the funeral. Said it was regimented. (I'm sorry. We did our best.) He stood at the grave and felt detached. "I'm not there," he said.

- He got excited again, saying something big is close. Something big, important, and good. He is planning over there. Spends time on it. He is close. Big, important surprises for the family. He is part of it.

The reading with Isabella was so healing. She is so kind and compassionate. She concluded with a comment that although Lee passed young, there was a completeness to his life. Somehow, I understand this.

Love, Mom

Friday, May 3, 5:30 a.m.

Dear Lee,

I greet the day outside. This is my favorite time. The birds are singing, woodpeckers going at the tree, and turkeys gobbling in the woods. I feel your tingles, on my head, letting me know you are with me. I heard a rooster in the distance. This simple start to the morning makes me happy. Is this what the next life will bring?

Love, Mom

Saturday, May 4

Dear Lee,

Today was Alana and Donald's wedding. I thought about you a lot and knew you were with us. I had the tingles to verify that. I sat and waited for people to approach me, but they didn't. Later, I realized I had an opportunity to teach them how grief is done, not be afraid to talk about someone's child, who has passed. Because that's what parents want. To talk about their kids. I let a teachable moment go by.

After the wedding, a few of us stopped by my brother's room. He had a little bar set up but forgot cups. Marisa (my niece) offered to go find some. As she stood to wait for the elevator, she heard a voice say, "Lee." She looked around, but there was no one in the hallway. I would love to have an audible experience like this, but I am happy that she had it.

Thank you,

Love, Mom

Sunday, May 5

Dear Lee,

I hadn't seen any hawks recently, so I asked for them today, then saw three. I gave JT your message today. I know that he is a super left-brained person, but he thanked me. He said that he always "looks up" when he talks to you in case you are there. I told him you are right here with us, not "up there," but I didn't push it I hope he will come around.

Love, Mom

Tuesday, May 7

Dear Lee,

I used to be so social. I loved being around people. At first, when you transitioned, I needed to be alone, to hurt, to process, and to find my way out of the early fog of grief. I understand the fog is a shock absorber from the reality of things you aren't ready to face. People want to help you at first. They bring you food, call you, or tend to you like a mother hen. But later, they mostly disappear. Then you feel abandoned, ostracized, and so alone. It's okay. I have greater hurts to heal.

Love, Mom

Wednesday, May 8

Dear Lee,

I haven't made much progress on our book. I know I'm procrastinating. Maybe it's just too big of a fear to overcome right now.

Love, Mom

Thursday, May 9

Dear Lee,

The quilts are done. I wonder if my blanket will bring me comfort or more pain.

Love, Mom

Friday, May 10

Dear Lee,

I'm here at the Omega Institute, for the retreat. This is the second Mother's Day without you. I'm grateful to be here with other mothers who understand. Twenty of us gather for the welcome and introduce ourselves. I feel you here with all the other mom's kids. I know that we are here for a reason. Jake Samoyedny is one of the mediums offering free readings. I hope to get a reading from him if it is meant to be. A nudge from you would be great if you agree.

Love, Mom

Saturday, May 11

Dear Lee,

The speakers and mediums all donated their time and talent this weekend. I got my reading with Jake. I understand spirit guides us to the right medium. I felt compassion and love from Jake. He said two people stepped in right away, the first had a quick illness—my dad. What happened next would have been enough for me to walk away satisfied. Jake knew your name. He saw his daughter, but heard, Lee. I think it's hard for mediums to get names, so I never expected it. He said your death was tragic, but you take ownership of it. I say, "Yes, he made a mistake." Jake said that you are smart. He knows I wonder how you could have been so careless. And you say, "Shit happens," which is funny. I can hear you saying this. Jake asks if others almost died. I tell him about Buddy. It would have been Summer, too, if she was still with you, but it wasn't her time. Jake asks if you were an introvert/extrovert. I say, "Yes. I understand this because I, too, am a deep thinker and live in my head. I need people to understand and challenge me, mind to mind. Just like you, I think." And I laughed as I heard, "Took you long enough."

Love, Mom

Sunday, May 12

Dear Lee,

No one wanted to leave Omega or each other. Saying goodbye was hard. I packed up, then sobbed all the way to my car, in the pouring rain. The tears cleansed me, on the inside, while the rain took care of the outside. This weather suits me, on this second Mother's Day with you on the other side of life.

I am grateful to everyone who brought us all together. I am grateful to Omega Institute for the provisions they provided. I am grateful to speakers who gave us so much love and hope. But most of all, I am grateful to you and the other kids, who guided their moms, to be there. A bond has been forged with this group, and I love them all. I look forward to seeing them again.

Love, Mom

Monday, May 13

Dear Lee,

My day was filled with 34's and hawk signs. This new way of communicating is real. How would I survive without this? So many parents suffer more than they should. You can't avoid the pain, but knowing the truth is everything.

Love, Mom

Tuesday, May 14

Dear Lee,

"All You Need is Love" comes on the radio in the car today, and I'm back at Christmas Eve, 2017. You wore your green sweater that night.

(Each year, I bought my grandkids and their cousins matching tee shirts. One year it was Rudolph and the next one, Grinch. And they would put on a little show, singing the appropriate song. But for some reason, in 2017, I bought "Be Kind" shirts, and we sang "All You Need is Love.")

There must be a reason.

Love, Mom

Wednesday, May 15

Dear Lee,

I had my Affiliate Leader orientation today. Afterward, I step outside to process. I asked you for a hawk to let me know this is the right thing. A short time later, I look up and there it is—one lone hawk circling high overhead. I take the sign.

Love, Mom

Thursday, May 16

Dear Lee,

When I was meditating, I imagined my heart as a gem being polished, and it was getting brighter. I will let my brilliance shine to help others. I ask all, on the other side, to guide, help, and heal me. Show me the way. Give me the knowledge and the strength to do the work. Walk with me, Lee. I need you. (tingles)

Love, Mom

Friday, May 17

Dear Lee,

I was in the car listening to an interview with Kerry McLeod and Philip Dykes. They mentioned my experience in Boston when I saw your image. And right at that moment, a hawk flies over the hood of the car. And tingles explode on my head. How incredible! I felt like I downed an energy drink. I was buzzed.

Love, Mom

Saturday, May 18

Dear Lee,

Thank you for so many hawks and 34's today, as we drove to Rochester. You are throwing the signs at me. I spotted five different hawks and eight 34's today. Stay connected, please.

Love, Mom

Sunday, May 19

Dear Lee,

Twenty-one years ago, my mom left this earthly life. She was only sixty-nine. It seemed so unfair. I wish I knew then what I know now about death and the afterlife, but I wasn't ready. I wasn't awake. But my eyes have opened since you left, and as hard as it is to understand and accept, I know there is a reason (tingles) and a plan, on a grander scale. I wish I could have learned these lessons some other way, but this is my path now, like it or not. I don't.

Love, Mom

Monday, May 20

Dear Lee,

I love that the hawk is your sign for me. I looked into their meaning. Hawks bring messages from the spirit world. It means the universe wants you to learn something. According to the Power of Positivity at the website: www.powerofpositivity.com, the hawk "symbolizes the ability to use intuition and higher vision, to complete tasks or make important decisions." My heart feels connected to these birds. I think they will help me to soar, to learn, to accept. Thank you for bringing these majestic beauties into my life.

Love, Mom

Tuesday, May 21

Dear Lee,

Our house is too quiet. I think back to the crazy days of raising kids. I miss it. I miss you. I would do it all over in a heartbeat.

Love, Mom

Wednesday, May 22

Dear Lee,

The quilts are done. I dread seeing them. I think the finality of your shirts being made into something else will hurt as much as it will help. It's like I was holding out hope that you were coming back to wear them, which I know is silly. I sometimes still pretend you are away on an extended business trip or living abroad to ease the pain. It helps for a moment.

Love, Mom

Thursday, May 23

Dear Lee,

I picked up the quilts. It was a huge trigger. I cried a lot. I can't look at them right now, so I left them in the car. I will wait until Memorial Day when the family gathers for a barbeque. I allowed the pain to rise and the tears to soothe

the ache inside me. Then I released my pain into the universe where it disappeared.

Love, Mom

Friday, May 24

Dear Lee,

Oddly enough, I feel calm. I can carry my pain today. I have no stress. No fears. No worries. The worse thing has already happened, so why worry? I can face anything now.

Love, Mom

Saturday, May 25

Dear Lee,

I meditated by the pond this morning. I asked you and everyone who loves me to step in. I immediately felt the tingles and slight pressure on my chest. It felt like a hug. I asked if it was you hugging me and heard, "We all are." Grateful and thankful.

Love, Mom

Sunday, May 26

Dear Lee,

God is good. It's 6:30 a.m., and I am sitting outside sipping coffee at our new campsite. The fish are jumping, the frogs are talking, and the birds are singing. I love this time of the morning as the world wakes up. I have a lot to be grateful for. And that's enough for today.

Love, Mom

Monday, May 27

Dear Lee,

Everyone will receive their quilts today. I think I'm ready now. I invited Ann to come to meet the family. These are precious mementos she has made for us. My quilt is a queen size, and the other four are lap quilts. These quilts were a labor of love, and I have a new appreciation for quilters. I will always hold a special place in my heart for Ann.

I know you will be with us today, but I asked for a sign. It was 12:05 p.m. when I saw the first hawk. We all saw two more during the barbecue, and I spotted the third after everyone left. It was a special day, and everyone loved the quilts, but I couldn't take a family picture. Not yet. The hole is still too glaringly obvious.

Love, Mom

Tuesday, May 28

Dear Lee,

My first Helping Parents Heal meeting is set for June 3 at the house. I'm taking baby steps, so I did not announce it publicly. I've invited some moms I know. There will be six of us.

Love, Mom

Wednesday, May 29

Dear Lee,

I looked at the clock three times this morning, at 8:34, 9:34, and 10:34. And I marvel at this.

I went to the restaurant where we celebrated your 30th birthday. I wasn't sure I could do it, but I actually felt comforted being in a place where we celebrated you. The only hurtful thing was the stupid comments people made. One said that God needed you more than me. I felt instant anger and thought, "How would you feel if God needed your child?" Then I felt bad and sent a silent apology to him. He doesn't understand. But I could have educated him that God doesn't "take" anyone. Believing this could make you angry, bitter, and turn away from God. The second person said he was surprised to "see me out." Am I supposed to stay in hiding, curled up in a ball, broken and ruined? I know this is not what you want, and I intend to make you proud.

Love, Mom

June 2019

Saturday, June 1

Dear Lee,

My soul was being tended to by angels, in meditation this morning. They were cleaning and polishing it like dental hygienists. I felt you nearby with my parents. You were all smiling and nodding, saying how good this cleansing is for me. I felt tingles on my head. I also felt the slight warm pressure hug, in my chest. It was an incredible feeling, and I cried, with the overwhelming feeling of love coming through from your side of life. I asked for a sign and later got my hawk. Thank you.

Love, Mom

Sunday, June 2

Dear Lee,

"Change is coming," popped into my head as I woke this morning. I turned to look at your picture, and I know. You want me to be happy. You want me to shine. To lead. To express joy. I will. I touch your quilt, and it gives me comfort—your life in a quilt.

Love, Mom

Monday, June 3

Dear Lee,

I held the first Helping Parents Heal meeting. A few moms said they almost changed their minds about coming, but came for my sake. I told them that they came because they were supposed to be there. I heard a story about an eighty-year-old mother who has buried three children. She sits all day looking at their pictures, waiting to die. And a father whose son was killed, on the highway, who drinks all day, hoping to die. People need to know there is a better way to do grief. People need to know life continues.

I said we will find ways to lift each other and turn our pain into purpose, as we work on our healing. Is there ever healing from child loss? I'm not sure, but we have to try.

Love, Mom

Tuesday, June 4

Dear Lee,

Two incredible experiences happened today. First, in meditation, I found myself floating in water with purple, green, pink, and orange colors bubbling up around me. I see a hallway, which leads somewhere even better than where I am, but I know I'm supposed to stay in the water. Then I realize that I'm not floating, but being supported by my angels. They are beautiful beings of bright light. I feel their love. I feel joy and peace. I know these beings are here to help me to heal me from the inside out. They have been holding me up since you crossed. They will be with me forever to show me the way. I hope I'm a good student. The lesson is simple because it's love. My tears start to flow. I have tingles, so I know this is true.

The second experience came during my Hawaiian massage today. I surrendered to the music and imagined I was on a beach, under a veranda. You were there, and we were drinking Coronas. I looked around and saw so many friends and relatives stretching back as far as I could see. It was as festive as a wedding reception. There were so many people I wanted to talk to. I thought, "How will I get to everyone?" They all laughed and said, "You already have." Thank you, God, for opening my heart.

Love, Mom

Thursday, June 6

Dear Lee,

I read about a young man who fell down the stairs at college like you and hit his head. He was on life support, and his parents had to make the horrible decision to turn it off. I'm glad I didn't have to make that choice. I didn't get to say goodbye, but I know you weren't alone. And I know you were escorted to the other side with love and greeted with even more love. Though I wish with all my heart you were here with me, I know all is well, and I take comfort in that too.

Love, Mom

Sunday, June 9

Dear Lee,

It's my second birthday without you. I'm down, but it's not as bad as last year. I know you are with me, but I would love a sign.

Dad and I went to a graduation party today, and I talked about you a lot. I want people to not be afraid to say your name. People's kids die, and we can't pretend otherwise. I was asked how I was doing. That's always a tricky question. I say I am doing the best I can. I explain I'm learning to carry my grief. It stays wrapped up deep inside me until I open and examine it. Sometimes you do it willingly, and sometimes it unwraps by itself. You don't expect it, but you accept it because this is your life now.

I didn't get my sign today, but that's okay. I probably wasn't paying attention.

Love, Mom

Tuesday, June 11

Dear Lee,

What happened today was no coincidence, no random act. Thank you, Lee, for bringing Reese and me together. You, no doubt, enjoyed watching the whole thing unfold.

(I was traveling to New Orleans to visit my cousin, Susie, who had recently lost her brother. A woman sat next to me, on the connecting flight. She mentions she's from Ft. Wayne and is going to New Orleans for a conference. I say my husband has been to Ft. Wayne for work. We discover they both work for BAE Systems, and she's been to Binghamton. When she tells me she's in contracts, I intuitively know that she knows Lee. "My son worked in contracts at BAE." "What is his name?" When I tell her, she looks shocked and says how sorry she is for my loss. It turns out that she knew Lee quite well. We spent the whole trip talking about him. We were meant to meet. When we parted, we hugged and promised to keep in touch.)

I don't know if you somehow arranged this today, but one thing is certain, it was no coincidence.

Love, Mom

Thursday, June 13

Dear Lee,

I was texting with a friend, and she asked if her healer could tune into me. I said yes, then suddenly felt a little woozy. It was a subtle feeling, and it passed quickly. The healer said I was good at self-healing, so she was just making some adjustments. Maybe this explains why I felt woozy. I feel like I'm blossoming to a whole new world. Then I hear "gift" and "feel your tingles." Can we settle for opportunity? I'm not ready to say "gift." But I am grateful for those helping me to grow and learn because without this journey, what would I have become? How else could I have survived this tragedy? The seed that was planted in me is beginning to grow. I know I have to tend it, love it and nurture it, to keep it alive. That's the hard part. It takes a lot of determination to nurture a garden, but I will.

At this point, Susie comes down from her bedroom and says, "I see you're using my diffuser." I said, "I didn't touch it." I hadn't even noticed the diffuser or that it was on until she mentioned it. Was that you, Lee? I will take it.

Love, Mom

Friday, June 14

Dear Lee,

I prayed to God to be open to whatever path I'm meant to be on. I prayed to accept the tools I need to carry out the job I am to do.

Love, Mom

Saturday, June 15

Dear Lee,

Today I will:

Open my heart to receive love.

Open my heart to receive peace.

Open my heart to receive compassion.

Open my heart to receive hope.

Open my heart to receive understanding.

Open my heart to receive healing.

Open my heart to feel joy.

Love, Mom

Sunday, June 16

Dear Lee,

It's Father's Day. I know Dad is sad. I can feel it. He doesn't share because he doesn't want to burden me with his pain. So, I imagined a golden thread from my heart to his during meditation and tried to energetically send love and healing to him. I wish I could take his pain. Please send him a sign today to give him some hope. Guide him to open to a new understanding. I pray for the gift of knowing for him and the whole family.

Love, Mom

Monday, June 17

Dear Lee,

We gave a $500 scholarship out, in your honor, at your high school. I talked about you and carbon monoxide. We brought 34 of them. They were all taken. You are helping.

Love, Mom

Tuesday, June 18

Dear Lee,

When I feel myself going back to January 2018, I try to replace it with a happy memory. I understand death is but a moment in a person's life. Your life was 30 years, 4 months and, 0 days or a total of 11,080 days. I will try to focus on the 11,079 days of your life, rather than the one day you left. Focus on what I had, not what I lost. And you existed before September 7, 1987, and you exist now. I know you are alive, well, safe, happy, and full of fun and joy. You are still the same person and still my Lee.

Love, Mom

Wednesday, June 19

Dear Lee,

I saw swirling colors during meditation. It was happiness, joy, and love mixed in with grief and pain. The positive feelings try to ebb away the grief, gently, slowly, and softly. I know I will never be free of pain, but it is softening. I've worked hard and will continue to do the work. I will do this for you. Don't worry about me. Just be happy, have fun, and wait for me. And communicate with me now and then.

Love, Mom

Friday, June 21

Dear Lee,

This day is starting rainy and gray, which suits me just fine. It's how I feel this morning. I try so hard, and I do believe, but it's still so hard. I am missing you so much right now. Despite the knowing, the sadness sneaks up without warning—unannounced and unwelcome. But that's how grief is. I have learned to live with it, perhaps even love it because it's part of me now. It has challenged me, stretched me into a new person. As I sit with my coffee and my journal, I feel the sadness lighten a bit. It is moving through and away for the time being. This is the ebb and flow of grief.

Love, Mom

Sunday, June 23

Dear Lee,

I know I will help myself by helping others. I hope I'm ready. I can manage my pain, but not sure that I can take on the pain of others. What is it that holds me back? Fear? And then I hear you say, "Jump off the cliff. You're going to land fine."

Love, Mom

Wednesday, June 26

Dear Lee,

I think about love today. You look at your newborn, and you are instantly in love. But if your child dies, that love is intensified beyond belief. There seems to be a thread of love that increases, but why? Is it the missing or longing for your child, or is it more? I think it might be God's way of showing us real love. A love that is ramped up when your child is physically gone from life. A vibration of love that increases until you go home, where you find the fullness of love. (tingles) The process of grief, the pain gives itself over to the love little by little. The pain, the grief can never be completely removed because how would the connection remain strong?

Love, Mom

Thursday, June 27

Dear Lee,

So many 34's today. Thank you. I got ready to leave for camp. It was 12:34 p.m. I ran errands and realized I forgot my key. Noticed the clock and it said, 1:34 p.m. Arrived at camp. It was 2:34 p.m. Picked up my phone to text Anna, and it was 3:34 p.m. Texted again, and it was 4:34 p.m. Then Jay texted me that he is home from vacation. It was 6:34 p.m. How does this all work?

Love, Mom

Sunday, June 30

Dear Lee,

Anna is 30 today. Exactly the age of your last earthly birthday. We are surprising her with a party. This family needs a celebration.

Love, Mom

July 2019

Thursday, July 4

Dear Lee,

I watched a small boy and his dad fishing today. A fresh wave of sadness washes over me as a memory of you fishing with dad pops up. I let my tears fall to soothe my sadness. The dad pulls out his phone, and I want to tell him to soak up the moment. Then the boy catches a fish, and it brings the dad back. I share in their joy.

Love, Mom

Friday, July 5

Dear Lee,

It was an amazing sign you sent me while I was lying in the hammock. Did you whisper in my ear, just in time, for me to look up from my book and see the cloud that spelled Lee? The L was backward, but it was clearly your name. I felt joy.

Love, Mom

Saturday, July 6

Dear Lee,

Today I will be grateful for my spiritual awakening.

Love, Mom

Sunday, July 7

Dear Lee,

I saw 34 hawks on our trip to Maryland. Every time I looked up from my book, there they were. At one point, there were a dozen of them together. Amazing. Thank you.

Love, Mom

Monday, July 8

Dear Lee,

I felt your presence in meditation this morning. Buddy was with you, and he jumped on my lap, which made me cry. He wouldn't have done this in his old life, but he isn't afraid now. I felt a warmth around me and heard, "I got you, Mom." Thank you, my beautiful son.

Love, Mom

Thursday, July 11

Dear Lee,

You were waiting for me on the bench, in the garden, in meditation. I can't see you, but I can feel you smiling. You told me to be fearless in writing our story, not to let doubt stop me. You said everything will unfold, as it will. My tears fell, and I felt the familiar tingles and warmth that lets me know you are with me.

Love, Mom

Friday, July 12

Dear Lee,

Today is Dad's birthday. Please let him feel you around.

Love, Mom

Saturday, July 13

Dear Lee,

I woke up with gratitude this morning. When I finished meditation outside, I looked around, and I felt connected to everything around me. I felt God in me and in all the things. I am awakening and unfolding. I see the truth and beauty of it all. And I'm grateful to notice, to be part of this.

Love, Mom

Sunday, July 14

Dear Lee,

"Life is what happens when you are busy making other plans" are the words I hear this morning. I will pay attention.

Love, Mom

Monday, July 15

Dear Lee,

Invites have gone out for the first annual LTN Memorial Golf Tournament. I feel good about this.

Love, Mom

Tuesday, July 16

Dear Lee,

Today I have gratitude for the two organizations that didn't respond to me after Ernie passed on. I'm not sure I would be in the place I am now. I've soaked up books, podcasts, and other teachings, like a sponge, allowing whatever feels

206

right to stick. Thank you, Lee, for guiding me to the right place and giving me the strength to go on. And thank you, God, for always loving me despite my doubts and fears. I am open to the truth. I accept.

Love, Mom

Wednesday, July 17

Dear Lee,

Surrender is my intention for my massage today. And I did. Sheehan said that she saw many points of light around me, as our guides worked together. I'm grateful for this healing work.

Love, Mom

Saturday, July 20

Dear Lee,

I watched a dad dance with his tiny daughter, at a winery today—a beautiful, simple pleasure for him, a painful trigger for me.

Love, Mom

Monday, July 22

Dear Lee,

As I woke this morning, I heard, "I had a beautiful life. It was just enough." I needed more.

Love, Mom

Tuesday, July 23

Dear Lee,

I saw a fleeting light out of the corner of my eye today. Do I trust it? Could it be you?

Love, Mom

Wednesday, July 24

Dear Lee,

I tried not to, but I asked the "why" question today. It's a question that can't be answered. It's pointless to ask. I decide to replace it with a gratitude litany.

I am grateful I had you for 30 years.

I am grateful you didn't suffer.

I am grateful you are having the time of your life.

I am grateful I am awakening to the truth.

I am grateful to God for all that I have.

I am grateful you will meet me when it's my time to return home.

Gratitude helps.

Love, Mom

Thursday, July 25

Dear Lee,

I saw two kids, near an ice cream store today, and gave them money, to get some ice cream. The boy jumped up and down like I had handed him gold. I think I was even happier than he was. I cried all the way home, then spotted a hawk. "We did good, Lee." Later, sitting outside, a hawk burst out of the woods and chased a bird off the feeder.

They came right under the patio about six feet from me. What a thrill. Thank you, Lee.

Love, Mom

Saturday, July 27

Dear Lee,

These words bring me hope today.

"I wouldn't come back for anything except to be with you. You can do anything. Go anywhere, be anything you want here. It's great. You'll see. Be patient. Do good. Be kind. Write the book." Soon after, I found two heart-shaped rocks. Thank you.

Love, Mom

Sunday, July 28

Dear Lee,

I wonder if things are too perfect on your side of life? If the temperature is perfect, you feel blissful, and nothing is ever wrong or bad, does it get a little boring? Is that part of the reason for souls to come here? It seems the more I learn, the more questions I have.

Love, Mom

Monday, July 29

Dear Lee,

While cleaning her closet, Hailey found a story she wrote five years ago. It was about the Cherokee Trail of Tears. She was on the trail with her family. She said everyone was sick: her mom, her dad, her two sisters (she only had one at this time). But the funny thing is, she said her Uncle Lee got sick and died. You were the only person to be named. Did she have a knowing? So interesting.

Love, Mom

Tuesday, July 30

Dear Lee,

I watched a homeless young woman approach an older woman in a parking lot, asking for money. The woman refuses, and the young woman turns away and starts to cry. It breaks my heart. She could be my daughter. She could be anyone's daughter. I call her over and ask her name. She tells me, Sara. She says she lives under the bridge with her husband, who will beat her up if she doesn't come back with enough money. It may or may not be true. It doesn't matter. But Sara does matter. I give her some money. Be safe, Sara.

Love, Mom

Wednesday, July 31

Dear Lee,

I was welcomed into a new group called Voices of our Angels by Ann Marie. Her son, AJ, also was born on September 7. And you were both golfers, though AJ was professional. Maybe you and AJ are golfing together. I don't know why, but I ask if she has or had a dog that was also born on September 7. I told her that you picked our beagle, Ruby, because she had the same birthday as you. Then Ann Marie says, "Oh my God. Our beagle/pug's name was Ruby." The world is full of synchronicities if you pay attention.

Love, Mom

August 2019

Thursday, August 1

Dear Lee,

Michael Jackson's "Man in the Mirror," pops into my head. I will work on seeing God in my mirror.

Love, Mom

Saturday, August 3

Dear Lee,

I felt you with Jesus in meditation this morning. I asked what you were doing, and you said, "Hanging. Learning." Jesus was dark-skinned with dark, curly hair and green eyes. I heard the song, "Hosanna," from Jesus Christ Superstar. I saw a bluish color I don't normally see in meditation. How is this even possible?

Love, Mom

Monday, August 5

Dear Lee,

Dad and I saw a hawk today that was low enough to see his shadow on the ground. It was thrilling. Thank you for the sign.

Love, Mom

Tuesday, August 6

Dear Lee,

Early on, I thought I lost me as well as you. Today, I realize it's no longer true. I liked myself before, but I like me even better now. I am more open and authentic. And I hear, "The price for love is more love."

Love, Mom

Friday, August 9

Dear Lee,

I am thinking about a tattoo again. beLEEve? Do the hawk and the tingles mean you approve?

Love, Mom

Saturday, August 10

Dear Lee,

I saw a woman walking on a country road today. She wore old, faded jeans and carried a purse. Not your typical jogger or walker. I passed her, then had a strong urge to go back. I ignored the feeling and kept going. Then I felt it stronger, and I heard, "Turn around and go back." So, I did. She told me that her daughter's house had burnt down that morning. She didn't have a car, so she was walking to town which was miles away. When I dropped her off, she said that she had no money, so I gave her all I had.

Love, Mom

Monday, August 12

Dear Lee,

I wrote these words during the night:

I'm meeting my grief head-on and facing this challenge with the fierceness, strength, and courage of a lioness protecting her cubs. And I will bear the scars of this battle with grace and honor until my life is completed, and I return to the home where I belong.

Love, Mom

Wednesday, August 14

Dear Lee,

It's funny how the wrong place turns out to be the right place. But I now understand that is how spirit works.

(I was trying to find a place that was having a meditation service and readings, only I didn't have an address, just a general location. I found a building, that I thought might be it, and walked in to find an older woman sitting there holding *A Course in Miracles* book. She said there wasn't a service being held there that evening. I said I must have the wrong place, and she replied, "Maybe you have the right place." She invited me to sit down. Rev. Carole had recently moved from New York City. She told me that she had been a fashion designer when her son passed twenty-five years before, sending her down a spiritual path. We ended up talking for two hours.)

I could learn a lot from this woman.

Love, Mom

Friday, August 16

Dear Lee,

We don't always like the gifts we are given, but we should accept them with grace and be grateful for them. I can accept the gifts of awakening, opening, and learning, but it will take time to be grateful for the way these gifts came to me.

Love, Mom

Sunday, August 18

Dear Lee,

I smelled coffee as I woke this morning. I thought Dad had gotten up and made some, but he was still asleep. Then I thought of my mom, which made me happy. I recently had a shared experience of smelling coffee with Aunt Kathy. No one loved coffee more than Grandma.

Love, Mom

Tuesday, August 20

Dear Lee,

My heart is heavy this morning. Even with all the knowing, the pain is real because the loss is real. But the love is also real. I hear, "I got you, Mom," and I feel a little better.

Love, Mom

Thursday, August 22

Dear Lee,

Did you unroll the 50/50 raffle tickets I set on the chair?

(I unwrapped and set a large roll of 50/50 tickets, on a chair. When I returned, it was unrolled three times. I was alone in the house, and the doors were closed, so there is no way that roll could have come undone without someone physically unrolling it.)

Love, Mom

Friday, August 23

Dear Lee,

This is my third time in Lily Dale. Spirituality is in the air here. I'm prepared for my reading with Jake Samoyedny. I hope I hear from you, but I will accept whoever has a message for me.

(Jake mentions several names I recognize and says they have gathered to listen. My mom and dad are the first to come in. My dad tells about almost drowning, at age eight, so I know it's him. Then Lee pulls closer, and Jake asks if he was a bit of a smart ass because Lee said, "Duh, asshole," in a mumble. It's Lee, for sure. Then he said, "It was me." Jake asks what he was referring to, and I tell him about the raffle tickets. Lee said he gets a kick out of the new electric bikes we have, but cautioned me to be careful or "You might end up over here with me." Lee thought it was funny that I was in Lily Dale, on Women's Weekend. I explained to Jake that in 2017, I had dressed up as a Suffragette and marched, in a centennial parade, in Binghamton. I found out that we are staying at an inn where Susan B. Anthony stayed, and Elizabeth Cady Stanton came to visit. I feel like I am in the right place at the right time. Lee showed Jake a blanket made from his clothes and says he likes that I wrap up in it and talk to him. Jake heard the names Ginger and Frenchie, which I do not recognize, but I will be open.)

Love, Mom

Saturday, August 24

Dear Lee,

I was surprised to learn the colors I see, in meditation, mean something. I assumed everyone saw colors, but I was told this is not the case. When I asked what the colors mean, I was told to ask my spirit guides. When I did, I heard, "Peace, love, surrender, serve." This is the most peaceful I have felt since you left. Does this mean I'm healing?

Love, Mom

Sunday, August 25

Dear Lee,

This weekend has been soul-enriching. I am grateful. It's hard to leave this place of peace and love, but I will be back next year.

Love, Mom

Monday, August 26

Dear Lee,

Tonight's Helping Parents Heal meeting went well. There were four of us. We talked about meditation and tried one for two minutes. Meditation has been integral to my healing.

Love, Mom

Tuesday, August 27

Dear Lee,

I have a secret garden inside of me where my grief lives. It's tended by angels, who lovingly care for it. But like any garden, my grief needs to be watered from time to time, so I take it out and give it the attention it needs. It will always be this way. It's a beautiful garden, full of the colors of love, kindness, and compassion, and you are always there waiting for me.

Love, Mom

Wednesday, August 28

Dear Lee,

I had a dream about you, but I am not sure if it was a dream visit or not. I watched the news as the New York Giants got off a plane. I spotted you for a split second and noticed you weren't in a uniform like everyone else. Later, I asked you why you weren't wearing a suit. You said, "I'm too small to play." I was secretly happy.

Love, Mom

Friday, August 30

In response to the letter I wrote to Lee on 8/6:

Dear Mom,

You ask if I am happy and having the time of my life, and the answer is yes. This is home, and I have just gone before you. And since there is no time here, then there is no separation between when I last saw you and when I will see you again. Try not to measure time. I am truly happy and don't feel cheated out of life at all. What happened was a preventable accident, but also an opportunity to exit, as was the case. Aren't you glad something worse didn't happen to me? Because it was going to happen. Things are not perfect here, at least in the way you think. It's not boring. I'm learning and growing here. I can do it because nothing is standing in my way, like work or other responsibilities. And as for communication, pay attention and be open. You miss a lot, you know. I have a life, so I can't send signs all the time. Keep on the path of growing and changing. You are doing great, and I am proud of you. I am with you always.

Love,

Lee

Saturday, August 31

Dear Lee,

The tournament is tomorrow, so Dad and Uncle Matt went to practice golfing. Uncle Matt unknowingly picked cart number 34, then Dad found a dime on the green. Then Jay tells me that as he was leaving his house, his TV came on all by itself.

Love, Mom

September 2019

Sunday, September 1

Dear Lee,

"Were you messing with your cousin tonight?"

(My 9-month-old nephew, Tommy, was sitting on my lap when he started wildly looking around like he was following something flying around the room. He was twisting from side to side and even arching backward. His mother, Marisa, said she had never seen him do anything like that before. She has a picture of Lee over his crib. No doubt, Tommy knew it was you, and I did too.)

Today was a day filled with love for you. There were tears and laughter. Many of your buddies came to play. It was the first time I saw how greatly affected they were by your death. I could see it in their eyes. I could see the love. I know you could see it too. But what happened tonight leaves no doubt in my mind that life continues, and you were with us today.

Love, Mom

Monday, September 2

Dear Lee,

What a beautiful synchronicity tonight. I was watching a movie called *Now and Then,* and a young girl is watching *Love Story* (1970 movie adapted from Erich Segal's book of the same name). It's at the part where Allie McGraw says, "Love means never having to say you're sorry." The movie ends, and I go back to Jake Samoyedny's book,

Gatekeeper of the Invisible Door, and there's the same line. This feels like a message from you. I promise I will do the work and be okay.

Love, Mom

Friday, September 6

Dear Lee,

I asked people on Facebook to do an act of kindness in honor of your birthday tomorrow. It's the best gift I can give to you.

Love, Mom

Saturday, September 7

Dear Lee,

Happy 32nd Birthday. I am grateful today for having you in my life for 30 years, but it wasn't enough. I think of the day you were born and how hard we both struggled to bring you into this world. It was a difficult day. It seems you left this world easier than you came in. I'm glad I got to spend your last birthday with you. It's a memory I will always cherish.

Love, Mom

Sunday, September 8

Dear Lee,

More words in the middle of the night:

Be open to the path before you. Let love and light illuminate this path. Don't be afraid to take the necessary steps. There is nothing to fear. Be like the hawk and soar with confidence. Fierce. Majestic. You, Lee, are my hawk, my guide. You light my path. Help me to not resist what is. Help me to surrender to the gifts.

Love, Mom

Wednesday, September 11

Dear Lee,

Growing up Catholic, I memorized prayers, studied Catechism, went to Communion and confession, but it was robotic. I didn't feel anything. I just went through the motions. I raised you Catholic, and I imagine it was the same for you. But my beliefs are changing, and what I am finding, feels right to me. The only truth is love and the service born out of that love. Gratitude helps you to see the gifts in your life. My flayed heart is ready to be infused with love.

Love, Mom

Thursday, September 14

Dear Lee,

Dad and I are in Phoenix for the Soul Summit conference. I am excited to soak up knowledge. I hope Dad can open a bit more. I also look forward to meeting my friend, Lisa.

Love, Mom

Friday, September 13

Dear Lee,

I sat outside in the Phoenix heat, for meditation this morning. I look at your picture and think, "This is for you," and you immediately correct me, "No, this is for you." I have to laugh because you are right.

I had an amazing sound healing today. I saw the sounds as ripples in water, which then changed to cube-like bursts of light. I thought I heard you call my name, but it was too far away to be sure. Always take the sign.

Love, Mom

Saturday, September 14

Dear Lee,

As I woke, I heard Stevie Wonder's song, "Joy Inside My Tears." I went outside with my coffee and listened to the song. You gave me joy for thirty years. How different my life would have been without you in it? What a surprise when Arizona Bell says you should ask two questions at the end of your life.

"Did you find joy?"

"Did you bring joy?"

I tell her about the song this morning, and it's no surprise, her dog's name is Stevie.

Love, Mom

Sunday, September 15

Dear Lee,

I didn't want the conference to end. The energy and love are so high and comforting here. It's easy to be around these people.

Love, Mom

Monday, September 16

Dear Lee,

We are in Sedona, and I watch the sun wake up the mountains. The air smells different here, piney and a bit like incense. We visited the Church of the Holy Cross. I lit a candle and prayed for all the children, who have left their parents, for the other side. Then I placed a dozen white roses for Amber (Lisa's daughter) whose ashes are by the lone tree there. We also went to the Amitabha Stupa and Peace Park. I wrote your name in the prayer book. Then I left my Helping Parents Heal stone, at the Buddha statue, for all the parents on this journey.

It was cloudy, so I didn't get to see the sunset, but I know I'll be back.

Love, Mom

Tuesday, September 17

Dear Lee,

My first glimpse of the Grand Canyon sent waves of emotion through me. I couldn't hold back the tears. When I am spirit, I will return here and fly over it like a hawk. Then I asked you for a hawk feather and heard, "Pay attention," so I will.

Love, Mom

Wednesday, September 18

Dear Lee,

I got my hawk feather today. It was not how I expected it, but the earrings are perfect.

Love, Mom

Thursday, September 19

Dear Lee,

I'm grateful for my suffering today. It's helping me to grow. I accept what I have been given to endure and the gift it brings. (tingles)

Love, Mom

Saturday, September 21

Dear Lee,

I don't have to like this new way to communicate, but I know it's real. I asked you for a butterfly today, and then after Ella and Ava's soccer game, a butterfly appeared. It circled the family ten or twelve times before it landed on Todd. Then it took off, circled, and again landed on Todd. I said, "Thank you, Lee," out loud and had immediate tingles on my head. Thank you, Lee, for letting us know you are with us.

Love, Mom

Monday, September 23

Dear Lee,

I saw a hawk and heard, "Freedom." Your freedom is my pain, but I am determined to be a shining light parent. I will take the hand of those behind me, who have been flung on this dark path.

Love, Mom

Wednesday, September 25

Dear Lee,

I wish you had realized how perfect you were. You were good enough. You didn't give yourself enough credit. You didn't believe in you. I wish I had put my arms around you and made you understand that.

Love, Mom

Friday, September 27

Dear Lee,

Truth made me cry today. It wasn't out of sadness, but one of knowing. Knowing that you exist. Knowing that you are happy. Knowing we will be together again. Knowing I have a purpose. Knowing I still have work to do. Knowing I have been given a gift. Knowing I can feel joy again. Thank you for helping me to know.

Love, Mom

Monday, September 30

Dear Lee,

I found the perfect place for the HPH meetings. Now I will prepare to announce. I know I have your support, but please send me a sign. Thank you for the hawks. (I first saw one, then two, then four hawks. Then there were ten of them.)

Love, Mom

October 2019

Wednesday, October 2

Dear Lee,

Sara channeled today. She spoke in a language I did not understand, but the gestures were ones of giving, and by the tone, I knew she was asking if I was ready to receive. I am.

Love, Mom

Friday, October 4

Dear Lee,

Joe McQuillen said he wouldn't want his son to feel bad watching his parents grieve when he existed in a place of joy, love and peace. I hadn't heard it put like that before. I would never want to cause you any anguish, on either side of the veil. No parent would want their child, in spirit, to feel bad witnessing their parent's grief. This is a good incentive to heal.

Love, Mom

Saturday, October 5

Dear Lee,

Dad was sad, thinking that you were missing Luke's opening football game today. Then he spotted two hawks and said he felt better. Thank you for showing him you are part of our lives.

Love, Mom

Sunday, October 6

Dear Lee,

How can I help the family find a spiritual path? "Example" is what I hear.

Love, Mom

Wednesday, October 9

Dear Lee,

I'm in the healing pool surrounded by angels, who cry healing tears into the wound that runs the length of my body. I feel the healing. I will carry a large scar. I will bear it like the warrior I am. I will wear it proudly because I have survived the worse thing a parent could ever endure. And I know you walk beside me on this path.

Love, Mom

Sunday, October 13

Dear Lee,

We left our campground today. It's been a peaceful retreat. I'm grateful for the time here, spent in quiet contemplation. Now it's time to move forward with the HPH group. I am blessed to do this work.

Love, Mom

Tuesday, October 15

Dear Lee,

I found a calendar from 1987. The day you were born was circled. Why did I save this calendar and no others? It feels like another piece of the jigsaw puzzle fell into place.

Love, Mom

Wednesday, October 16

Dear Lee,

You tell me it's Italy today. I love that you can go anywhere. And even if you don't go, I'm happy you play this game with me.

Love, Mom

Sunday, October 20

Dear Lee,

I woke up with the song "G.T.O." Maybe you and Grandpa are riding around with big smiles, laughing, screaming with the wind blowing in your hair.

"C'mon and turn it on, wind it up, blow it out, GTO."

Pick me up when I cross.

Love, Mom

Tuesday, October 22

Dear Lee,

I'm not sure where Burma is, but it's the adventure today. You didn't like traveling when here, but maybe now that it's hassle-free, you are game. I'll go places with you once I'm there. "Mom, start to travel," I hear. I may be ready.

Love, Mom

Wednesday, October 23

Dear Lee,

Reverend Pat said I'm doing God's work. I didn't think about it like that. It makes me want to do my best, even if it scares me a little.

I saw several 34's and a hawk today. Confirmation that all will be well.

Love, Mom

Thursday, October 24

Dear Lee,

My cousin's son is dead. I know he is home free, being tended to, loved and healed, from the pain and difficulties he endured in this life. I know his grandmother helped him to cross, my beautiful aunt, who buried four of her eleven children plus two husbands. I promised them I will be there for my cousin. I know what she now faces.

Love, Mom

Saturday, October 26

Dear Lee,

When I heard "Ukraine" this morning, I knew I had to forgive Todd and April's father for abandoning them. I have to trust this was the plan. I will write a letter of forgiveness that I won't send. I will forgive myself, too. I need to do this for my soul.

Love, Mom

Monday, October 28

Dear Lee,

Shirts, in your honor, have been designed for the annual Thanksgiving flag football game. I heard, "Make him play." I knew you meant Jay. I answered, "I can't make him play, Lee." And I heard again, "Make him play. He needs to play. For me." I hope he can.

Love, Mom

Tuesday, October 29

Dear Lee,

My friend Elaine's nephew passed from an overdose. Another young person. She said he was the son she never had. Her heart is broken like every parent who has to endure a devastating loss like this. I wish no one had to make the journey down this path. My heart aches for them all.

Love, Mom

Wednesday, October 30

Dear Lee,

It seems impossible you left me 661 days ago, and I hear, "I didn't leave you. I just left." I wonder how many years will stretch out until I am with you? Ten, twenty, thirty? I know from your perspective, it's just a blink. Well, I'm blinking, but I'm still here, so I guess it will be awhile.

Love, Mom

November 2019

Friday, November 1

Dear Lee,

Dad and I decided to go to a burger place tonight. As we neared the restaurant, I said, "I'm not feeling it. Let's go Mexican." We pulled into the parking lot, and a Mexican song came on the radio. It wasn't until we went inside that we realized it was the Day of the Dead, a day to honor and celebrate those, who have passed, not like the All Souls Day last year, which made us sad.

Love, Mom

Saturday, November 2

Dear Lee,

In a semi-waking state this morning, I saw mountains and stars with lots of colors. I saw a hand reach out, and for some reason, I thought of John Lennon. Maybe you are at a concert having the time of your life.

Love, Mom

Sunday, November 3

Dear Lee,

I missed your physical presence at the family breakfast this morning. I miss the banter with your siblings. I miss you playing with your nephew and nieces. This will never change.

Love, Mom

Tuesday, November 5

Dear Lee,

"See what you got me into?" is what I sometimes say when I think about the road ahead. This is not the retirement I expected. I guess the universe had different plans for me.

Love, Mom

Wednesday, November 6

Dear Lee,

How interesting that I met a mom from the HPH group in yoga today. It was her first time at yoga. When she said her name, my gut told me it was her. After class, we went for coffee. Spirit has perfect timing.

Love, Mom

Thursday, November 7

Dear Lee,

I woke up with the song line, "I want you to be happier" and heard "Alaska." Are you telling me that it's time? Maybe in a year or two.

(I had planned on going to celebrate my retirement in 2018 before Lee passed.)

Love, Mom

Friday, November 8

Dear Lee,

"It pisses me off," I heard Dad mutter, as he was cleaning the fireplace. I knew what he meant, but I wanted him to say it, so I asked what he was talking about. "We didn't clean Lee's furnace. I never thought of it. I assumed he took care of it." I don't know if he will ever forgive himself. I wish he understood there is nothing to forgive.

Love, Mom

Saturday, November 9

Dear Lee,

Once I was ignorant of pain. I suffered things like anyone else, but I didn't know pain on such a deep, personal level until I lost you. Pain and I are now well-acquainted, but I don't want to be best friends.

Love, Mom

Sunday, November 10

Dear Lee,

I felt your presence the most I have in meditation. I could feel the warmth of you wrapped around me and a squeeze from the inside out. Tears fall. They weren't sad ones. They were emotional ones, not quite joy, but powerful and beautiful. I had tingles the whole time, then I felt you pull away, out of the top of my head. I didn't want it to end. Thank you for being with me.

Love, Mom

Tuesday, November 11

Dear Lee,

I started to type an email today, and your college email popped up. I haven't used that email since you graduated, almost ten years ago, so it was a surprise. I typed, "I love you and miss you" and sent it. Then I felt tingles. I'm glad you got my email.

Love, Mom

Wednesday, November 12

Dear Lee,

What do people see when they look at me? They see my shell, but not the real me. What do they think? I'm better, healed, strong? Do they see the pain I carry in my heart? Do they know the constant work I do? It doesn't matter what they think because I know the truth. I am a shining light parent.

Love, Mom

Thursday, November 13

Dear Lee,

My first meeting, at the church, was tonight. Twenty-three people walked through the door. The meeting went okay at first, but then it spiraled down. The goal is for people to leave feeling uplifted. People need to share their stories, but this is not a grief group, and I am sure not a counselor. I will find the balance.

Love, Mom

Friday, November 14

Dear Lee,

A little self-care was in order today.

Love, Mom

Monday, November 18

Dear Lee,

I'm feeling the pull of the rabbit hole today. Maybe I can dip my toe in, but not fully immerse. It must be the upcoming holidays, pulling me toward the edge. It's only the second Thanksgiving without you physically present, so I know I am still early in grief. But I don't want to focus on you being missing. I want the focus to be presence, not absence.

Love, Mom

Tuesday, November 19

Dear Lee,

I know you are happy I'm hosting Thanksgiving. I don't want to, but I will for you. It will be my last one.

Love, Mom

Wednesday, November 20

Dear Lee,

Uncle Dan told me that you poured a little beer, on the ground, at the last Thanksgiving. When he asked why, you said, "It's for everyone who is not with us." We are planning on burning some of your papers, as a symbolic offering to you, so maybe we will also make a toast.

Love, Mom

Friday, November 22

Dear Lee,

I'm having second thoughts about Thanksgiving. I'm afraid it will be too much for us. And I hear, "Presence not absence." I want to make that the focus, but I'm not sure I can. I could use a sign.

Love, Mom

Saturday, November 23

Dear Lee,

I saw 15 redheads today. Who sees that many in one day? Thank you for the reassurance.

Love, Mom

Sunday, November 24

Dear Lee,

New Zealand is my first thought this morning. I look it up and learn the South Island's Fiordland and Southern Lakes stood in for Middle Earth in Peter Jackson's *Lord of the Rings* films. You must have loved it there.

Love, Mom

Monday, November 25

Dear Lee,

Dad thinks burning your things might be too much for the family right now, so we decided not to do it at this time. I hope that's okay. We will have the toast. I know you will like that.

Love, Mom

Wednesday, November 27

Dear Lee,

I am grateful for my guardian angels and guides who have taken care of me all my life. I know it wasn't always an easy job. I need their help right now and yours too. Please help me get through Thanksgiving.

Love, Mom

Thursday, November 28

Dear Lee,

I sat with my coffee this morning. After meditating, I set my phone down, and a video of you pops up. I laughed and cried. How does this happen? I don't know, but I hope this is a sign dinner will go well.

Love, Mom

Friday, November 29

Dear Lee,

I was so disappointed with Thanksgiving. It went exactly as I expected but hoped it wouldn't. I had hoped that everyone would share stories about you, but it didn't happen. The kids wrote beautiful notes and decorated a little Christmas tree for you, which made me happy. Later, after everyone was in bed or had left, Matthew (Lee's first cousin) sat and held my hand while I talked and cried. He listened. It helped me a lot. I could feel you near. He is deep and caring. I am grateful for the love and kindness he showed me.

Love, Mom

Saturday, November 30

Dear Lee,

During a guided meditation, on forgiveness, this morning, I heard Jesus' words, "Forgive them for they know not what they do." I realized I let myself be disappointed over something my extended family doesn't understand. They couldn't possibly, and I wouldn't want them to know, much less, feel the pain of this kind of loss. I let it go.

Love, Mom

December 2019

Sunday, December 1

Dear Lee,

I'm having a reading with another medium today. I meditated and asked you to come, but I will accept who needs to give me a message. I put on some Stevie Wonder to raise my vibration, and when I glance at the clock, it says 11:11. Wow. I could feel spirit drawing close. I felt tingly and excited. Everyone was ready on both sides.

- She felt toxins in the body with a bad pain in the head.
- She recognized some anxiety, depression, and a lack of self-confidence.
- She saw someone with a cut on the forehead, at the hairline, that received staples. (Jay cut his head on a malfunctioned weight machine in 2002.)
- She saw a large dog that slept in its own human bed. (We adopted a Great Dane, in the early '90s. She came with a twin bed.)
- She heard "Bippety Boppity Boo" and saw the fairy godmother changing Cinderella's dress with a wand. (This is Lee teasing Jay. It was his favorite part of the movie when he was little.)
- She saw a little car with a number 12 on it. (Matchbox found by Tom in the garage and first mentioned in a reading by another medium.)
- She saw a small wren-like bird. (I bought a cockatiel a few months after Lee passed.)

- She says Lee is pushing forward a young man who was murdered. He said to tell his mom, "I'm safe." (My friend's missing son. I pass it along.)

These are things she could not possibly know. And it proves beyond any doubt, you are alive and well.

Love, Mom

Monday, December 2

Dear Lee,

"Was I a good mom, Lee?"

"The perfect one. I picked you, remember?"

I picture you and Ernie standing together, beaming with pride. Ernie says, "You're way ahead of the curve, kid." I understand what this means now. I'm grateful for the few months I spent with this special man. I hope he is having the time of his life, too.

Love, Mom

Tuesday, December 3

Dear Lee,

German words woke me up during the night. It could only be Fritz (my writing guide). I didn't understand the words, but the tone was stern. Is he telling me to finish the book? I feel Fritz wears the traditional Lederhosen. He is a bit of a curmudgeon, but I feel his love.

(We now have a Miniature Schnauzer puppy, named Fritz. I know Lee chose him for us. On January 24, during meditation, I saw a Schnauzer-type dog. When I told Tom about it, he said he had been researching dogs, the day before, and was drawn to the Schnauzer. He thought he might surprise me for my birthday in June. Curious, I went online and found a local breeder. I was drawn to one little face, out of all the puppies. Then after the third visit to the site, I realized this particular pup was available, for a home, on the day Lee had passed. We couldn't deny Lee brought Fritz into our lives, and he has brought so much love and joy.)

Love, Mom

Thursday, December 5

Dear Lee,

I feel a change deep within me—a trauma-induced spiritual awakening. I will always miss you, but I no longer miss me. If that's the gift, I accept.

Love, Mom

Friday, December 6

Dear Lee,

I went to the meditation garden. Grandma was there. She told me how proud she is of me. I never communicated with my mom like this before. I tell her I'm not sure I can lead this HPH group. She tells me I have to because people need me. I ask, "Why me?" She says I must be the leader I have always been. Then I hear the Mickey Mouse theme song. I smile because I know it's my dad chiming in. When I was little, my dad would come home from work and tell me to look in his shirt pocket to see what Mickey Mouse brought me. He would always have some little treat or trinket in there. Thank you, Dad, for the spot of humor in my moment of doubt and fear.

Love, Mom

Saturday, December 7

Dear Lee,

When you told me today you were not going to live past 40 and you just "scooted out" a little early, I knew this was really you. I could not make this up. And I would never say that. This is the strongest validation I've had yet.

Love, Mom

Sunday, December 8

Dear Lee,

Dad and I went to a candle-lighting service tonight for parents who have lost children. We did not like it. It was too somber and depressing. Where was the celebration of our kids' lives? The only highlight of the service was when the man behind us set his Santa Claus-like beard on fire. As he was furiously patting out his beard, I wondered if maybe you had caused that little scene. I had a hard time suppressing my giggles. Next year, I will light my own damn candles!

Love, Mom

Monday, December 9

Dear Lee,

Grief is so fickle.

Love, Mom

Wednesday, December 11

Dear Lee,

Texas is what I heard when I asked where you are exploring today. "Why Texas?" "Riding bulls," is what you said. This game is fun. Thank you for playing.

Love, Mom

Thursday, December 12

Dear Lee,

My second HPH meeting is tonight. I will leave a seat empty beside me. Please be there.

Love, Mom

Friday, December 13

Dear Lee,

The second meeting went well. A local medium came, and everyone received a message. The energy in the room was high. There were smiles and hugs, and everyone left feeling uplifted. I was so relieved.

Love, Mom

Saturday, December 14

Dear Lee,

I heard "Warsaw, Poland" this morning. You must be learning and experiencing so much. I am proud of everything you are doing on your side of life, just as I was when you were physically here.

Love, Mom

Sunday, December 15

Dear Lee,

I felt wrapped in love during meditation this morning. I felt brushes, tingles, and chills. I know it's everyone who loves me.

Love, Mom

Monday, December 16

Dear Lee,

Was that you interrupting the HPH zoom meeting I was in tonight? (There was a screeching noise at least three times, and it's been happening a lot lately.) No one, in the meeting, mentioned this happening, so I assume it was just on my end. Does this mean I have to find it amusing rather than annoying?

Love, Mom

Thursday, December 19

Dear Lee,

Our family took part in a YWCA holiday program. We bought gifts for two young kids, in your honor. We gave the mom a gift card for food and a carbon monoxide detector, in case she didn't have one. I imagined the kids' excitement on Christmas morning. How I miss those Christmas mornings. I would do it all over again, even knowing the outcome. I miss you.

Love, Mom

Friday, December 20

Dear Lee,

I'm in the garden, but it's my guardian angel, Rhonda, in there, not you. She says, "Let's take a walk." I notice the colors change as we walk by the different flowers. I see so many people, but I'm most surprised to see my old friend, Robin, who passed decades ago. In the distance, I spot Jesus speaking with a group. I don't care if this is real or my imagination, I love this place.

Love, Mom

Saturday, December 21

Dear Lee,

As I started on a short out-of-town trip today, I had a vision of an accident with a truck, and I couldn't go. Later, April told me about a near-miss she had on the highway. She was following a truck with an unsecured couch in the back. It was bouncing around, and she knew it was going to come out. Then just as she passed the truck, the couch lifted out and tumbled along the highway. If she hadn't passed the truck, the couch would have hit her. I like to think you kept her safe.

Love, Mom

Tuesday, December 24

Dear Lee,

I woke in the night when I heard *"Sophie's Choice."* I hadn't had that thought in a long time, but it no longer scares me. I know now I didn't single you out as I thought in the beginning. (I had reoccurring nightmares thinking this.) I understand it was an agreement for you to leave before me, to grow my soul. And I am.

Love, Mom

Wednesday, December 25

Dear Lee,

There's a fine line between living in the past and cherishing the memories. I'm trying to cherish it, but today, I want to go back. It's Christmas, and all I want is you. I feel myself sinking. I try to focus on what this day is about. I think of Jesus given, as a gift, to the world to teach us how to live, but we don't hear. I think of Mary suffering the loss of her gift, and I know her pain. And I think you, too, were a precious gift given to me and the world for thirty years and I am grateful.

Merry Christmas, Lee.

Love, Mom

Tuesday, December 31

Dear Lee,

In this new year, I resolve to walk the path of kindness, love, compassion, and forgiveness because nothing else matters.

Love, Mom

January 2020

Wednesday, January 1

Dear Lee,

Today I start a new year on a path I can't see. Please help me stick to the path and not get lost in the woods. I trust the guidance and wisdom will be there as I travel.

Love, Mom

Saturday, January 4

Dear Lee,

I try to imagine the beauty of your side of life. I know it will be so much fun there, but I know, for now, my work is here. I no longer ask "why" because I know I won't have the answers until I arrive home. For now, I will work on my spiritual growth and be the best person I can.

Love, Mom

Monday, January 6

Dear Lee,

As your second-anniversary approaches, I'm crumbling. As soon as I entered the garden in meditation, you took me in your arms, and I sobbed. I asked you why, and you said, "It just is." "I don't want it. It's too hard," I told you. We sat on a bench. You held my hand and told me I'm doing everything right. Then I asked God to infuse me with healing light and love to help me through the next few days.

Love, Mom

Tuesday, January 7

Dear Lee,

Today is the day you passed. This will always be the day I hold in my heart, not the awful day of discovery. I put an ad in the newspaper to honor you:

In Loving Memory of Lee Thomas Norris

Missing you every moment of every day, but

honoring you with every breath in every way.

beLEEve

Spirit was around in meditation. I could feel their love. It's why I can be okay today. It doesn't mean I don't have pain, and I won't cry from the ache of missing you, but I can carry it a lot easier than if I hadn't done this work. It's constant work, but I know life goes on in a different, but more real way. My life here is temporary, and we will be together again. I will hold on.

Love, Mom

Wednesday, January 8

Dear Lee,

The family sent up sky lanterns with love to you last night. I wrote "beLEEve" on each one. And I do.

Love, Mom

Thursday, January 9

Dear Lee,

It's been two years since our life-shattering discovery. I don't want to think back on the details of the day, but I wonder if I should? Am I avoiding the pain by not reflecting on the day? And I hear you say, "It serves no purpose." And you are right. I've worked too hard and learned too much to dismantle it by jumping into the pit of despair. I know the truth. You are alive and well. Knowing this doesn't make me miss you any less, but it does make me love you more. And I can be okay knowing you are happy and loving the life you are now living. And I know you will be with me always.

Love, Mom

Lee's Favorite Recipes

New England Clam Chowder

Lee's submission for a Cultural Cookbook in eighth grade.

New England Clam Chowder

Ingredients:
2 dozen medium-size quahog clams (or frozen/canned clams)
½ pound salt pork, minced, 4 cups diced potatoes
½ cup chopped onion
2 cups milk
1 cup light cream.
3 tablespoons all-purpose flour

Happy Holidays
Lee Norris

Directions:
Scrub clams. Cover with salt water (½ cup salt to 1 gallon water);
let stand 15 minutes; rinse. Repeat twice. Remove clams and dice,
reserving ½ cup liquor. Fry pork till crisp; remove bits of pork,
reserve. Add ½ cup liquor, 1½ cups water, potatoes and onion to fat.
Cook covered 15 to 20 minutes. Add clams, 1½ cups milk and
cream. Blend ½ cup milk and flour, stir into chowder. Heat to
boil; stir occasionally. Add 1½ teaspoons salt and dash pepper. Top
with pork. Serves 10.

Hummus

Put all ingredients in a food processor.

1 can of garbanzo beans, drained and rinsed.

2 tablespoons olive oil

2 tablespoons lemon juice

2 tablespoons water

2 tablespoons tahini (sesame paste)

2-3 cloves garlic

Salt to taste.

Process until smooth. Add a little more oil if necessary.

Serve with pita chips and/or raw vegetables.

Afterword

For two years, I've been strapped on a roller coaster ride of emotion. I had no choice but to hang on and ride the ride. It's a wild ride, but I have learned so much. I have learned that life continues. We come here to learn lessons, and it's the tragedies that bring us the most valuable ones. I have learned to go deep in meditation, to the core of me. I have come to sense and know my angels and guides. I have learned to trust the signs and messages I receive from Lee, especially the ones that drop-in, during the night, or as I'm waking.

(For example, Lee told me to put his favorite recipes in the book.)

"Thank you, Lee. That's brilliant."

However, the most important lesson I have learned is that we are all one with God, and love is the glue that binds us. Forgiveness, kindness, gratitude, and compassion are the keys to unlock that love.

I would do anything to have Lee here with me physically, but I can't change that. I have no choice but to live with the pain of my child leaving this world before me. I do, however, have a choice in what I do with that pain. I can reject or accept the gift the pain has brought me. I accept.

I am a work in progress. My soul is like a piece of art being stretched, shaped, and molded into a thing of beauty. The process is slow, and the work is hard, but it is what I will do for the rest of my life.

Lee had a purpose while here on earth, and he has a purpose now. He continues to live, love, grow, expand, guide, and learn, in a place called home. I know he is limitless beyond time but still connected to everyone here he loves. What else would keep me bound to this earth? So, I accept my pain, as the price for love. I will carry it as a precious gift, wrapped in my heart. And I vow to live the rest of my life, as best I can, while I wait for the day when Lee comes to escort me home.

I beLEEve!

Christmas 2016

Acknowledgments

I am forever grateful for each person on this list who has helped me, on this journey, in some way. I wouldn't be where I am without them.

Thank you to the following:

My family

Dr. Eben Alexander (ebenalexander.com)

Elizabeth Boisson, Co-founder, and president of Helping Parents Heal (helpingparentsheal.org)

Sandra Champlain (wedontdie.com)

Cynthia Campbell and the Omega Institute (Desiree's Gathering)

Caroline Chang (awake2onenessradio.org)

Rev. Dr. Teri Daniel (danieldirect.net)

Sara Ann Delafield (RedfeatherRetreat.com)

Suzanne Giesemann (suzannegiesemann.com)

Roberta Grimes (robertagrimes.com)

Isabella Johnson (thesoulreadingmedium.org)

Lisa Laniewski

Dr. Mary Neal (drmaryneal.com)

Ann Van Orsdel (annvanorsdel.com)

Sonia Rinaldi (afterliferesearch.org)

Christine Salter (christinesalter.com)

Jake Samoyedny (compassionatemedium.com)

Jane Seybold (janeseybold.com)

Kyra and Todd Schaefer (asyouwishpublishing.com)

Brian Smith (grief2growth.com)

Susanne Wilson (thecarefreemedium.com)

Irene Vouvalides, Vice President of Helping Parents Heal

Thank you to the many authors for the beautiful books you wrote that gave me the knowledge and the will to go on.

And a very special thanks to my good friend, Deb Johnson, who stood by me, showering me with love and support. I love you, dear friend.

I am also grateful to those in the hereafter who have nudged and guided me along the way:

God

Lee

Harriet

Fritz

Rhonda

My parents

About the Author

Rosanne Groover Norris was born in Johnson City, New York, where she grew up with five siblings. She is married to Thomas Norris and is the mother of five children and six grandchildren. They are her best accomplishments in life. She has a Bachelors in English from Binghamton University, where she spent her career working at the University's Performing Arts Center.